Here's what oth…
say about Self-…

"Compelling. Candid. Controversial. You have to read it!"

Steve McDermott. Former European Business Speaker
of the Year and bestselling author

"You will love this book. Paul McGee is an incredibly intuitive and inspiring presenter and writer. This book will go a long way in helping you regain and rebuild your confidence so that you can reach your full potential for your life."

Rosemary Conley CBE. Diet and Fitness Guru

"From improving your love life, to boosting your job prospects, confidence can unlock the doors to a brighter future. This brilliant book, packed with honesty, humour and hope, provides the keys."

Laine Ferguson. Retail Director of The Body Shop

"Packed with practical ideas and insights to build your confidence from the boardroom to the bedroom – and most things in between. You'll wish you'd read this book years ago."

Philip Hesketh. Award winning, international speaker
and best selling author

And what they say about Paul McGee, The *SUMO* Guy:

"Your input made an incredible difference. The average score of how well people felt able to cope with change, moved from 71% to 94%; a great move, especially starting from a reasonable base. Your SUMO ideas continue to be frequently used."

Marks & Spencer

"May I on behalf of everyone at Manchester United who attended your session, thank you for a great presentation. The feedback has been excellent and all very positive and I know the ideas within your S.U.M.O. message are greatly appreciated."

Kenneth Merrett, Manchester United F.C.

"In our twenty years of running conferences, Paul McGee is the only speaker we have ever invited back. That above all, explains the benefit we feel we have gained from hearing Paul's SUMO philosophy."

Doug Perkins & Dame Mary Perkins CBE,
Founders of SpecSavers

"Paul you're not a motivational or inspirational speaker .... I actually think you're a life-changing speaker. You give people the tools to change their lives."

Nigel Risner, Television Presenter and Speaker

"Dear Paul, Just wanted you to know that I found your SUMO book both stimulating and instructive. The world of business moves on at such a pace that I believe the SUMO ethos is an essential part of the buiness person's DNA."

Lord Digby Jones

"Every organisation these days needs to be looking for value for money ... we made an investment in over 2,500 of our staff attending a SUMO seminar with Paul McGee. Staff were given insights and ideas that could help them be more effective at work, deal more positively with the challenge of change, and build better relationships with both the public and colleagues. The overwhelming feedback has been that the sessions were inspiring, thought-provoking, humorous but above all practical in helping my staff make a positive difference. I would have no hesitation in recommending Paul McGee and his SUMO philosophy to any organisation."

Julie Spence, Chief Constable, Cambridgeshire Police

Other books by Paul McGee, The SUMO Guy:

S.U.M.O. (Shut Up, Move On®): The Straight Talking Guide to Creating and Enjoying a Brilliant Life

S.U.M.O. Your Relationships: How to Handle not Strangle the People You Live and Work With.

Both published by Capstone Publishing

www.thisiscapstone.com

Follow Paul McGee on Twitter@TheSumoGuy or visit www.TheSumoGuy.com

Self-Confidence

About the Author

Paul McGee is one of the UK's leading speakers on the areas of change, confidence, workplace relationships and motivation. His thought-provoking, humorous and practical approach to life's challenges has seen him speak in 35 countries to date and he is the author of seven books. He is also a personal life coach working with one of the English Premiership's leading teams.

The proud creator of SUMO (Shut Up, Move On), his simple yet profound messages have spread across the globe both in public and private sector organisations. More recently his ideas have been developed for young people under the banner of SUMO4Schools.

Building on his academic background in behavioural and social psychology, Paul is also a trained counsellor, a performance coach and a Fellow of the Professional Speaking Association. His aim is simple – "I want to help people achieve better results in life and have more fun in the process". For more information visit www.TheSumoGuy. com or follow Paul on Twitter: @TheSumoGuy.

Self-Confidence

Second Edition

The Remarkable Truth of Why a Small Change Can Make a Big Difference

Paul McGee

Illustrations by Fiona Griffiths

CAPSTONE

Library of Congress Cataloguing-in-Publication Data
McGee, Paul, 1964-
    Self-confidence : the remarkable truth of why a small change can make a big
difference / Paul McGee.—2nd ed.
        p. cm.
    ISBN 978-0-85708-287-9 (pbk.)
    1. Self-confidence. 2. Self-actualization (Psychology) 3. Success—Religious
aspects. I. Title.
        BF575.S39M36 2012
        158.1—dc23

                                                                        2011044009

A catalogue record for this book is available from the British Library.

ISBN 978-0-857-08287-9 (pbk) ISBN 978-0-857-08298-5(ebk)
ISBN 978-0-857-08300-5 (ebk) ISBN 978-0-857-08299-2(ebk)

Set in 11/14 Baskerville Classico by Toppan Best-set Premedia Limited
Printed in Great Britain by TJ International Ltd, Padstow, Cornwall, UK

To Matt and Ruth

"Chickahelameni"

With love

From

Your Mad Dad

Contents

About the Author   **vii**
Preface to the 2nd Edition   **xv**
Introduction   **1**

SECTION ONE: The Stuff You Need to Know   **9**

1   Why Self-Confidence is the X-Factor for Life   11
2   Taking the "Con" Out of Confidence   29
3   Who Crushed Your Confidence?
    Your Upbringing   47
4   Who Crushed Your Confidence?
    Other Influences   75

**SECTION TWO: The Stuff that Will
Really Help**   **95**

5   You'll Get By with a Little Help from
    Your Friends   97
6   How to Be Your Own Best Mate   123
7   How to Shine When Your Neck's on the Line   151
8   What to Do When the Ship Hits the Flan   197
9   How to Handle Conflict Confidently   223
10   Have You Got the Confidence to Go M.A.D.?   249

How it Worked for Me   **269**
More Stuff That Will Help   **277**
Time for Some Gratitude   **279**
Bring Paul McGee to Your Organisation   **283**
Index   **285**

Preface to the 2nd Edition

Well I guess if you're reading a book about self-confidence you would expect the author of such a title to be brimming over with bucket loads of the stuff.

Well if I'm honest that's not always how I feel.

When it comes to writing about the subject matter I do feel confident. I have a supportive editorial team and friends who pull no punches when it comes to giving me feedback on my content.

So was I confident about what I'd written?

Absolutely.

But was I confident the book would sell well?

I was hopeful and expectant but not totally confident.

Maybe that's not such a bad thing.

A little self-doubt is a good weapon against complacency and arrogance.

You see, it's only when you see the actual sales figures that any grounds for optimism can be justified.

Hence I felt like a child on Christmas morning waiting to hear the initial sales figures.

I was ecstatic when they came through.

Clearly self-confidence was and still is a big issue for lots of people.

And I'm going to make a small confession. I'm sure it's one most authors relate to but one they rarely admit.

It's simply this:

The overwhelming sense of satisfaction they experience when they find their book prominently displayed in a bookstore.

What could be better than that?

Well actually there is something.

When you're proudly staring at your book in a bookstore and then someone reaches past you to pick up a copy. The tension and excitement is I confess almost overwhelming.

As is the inner struggle.

Do I or do I not strike up a conversation with this unsuspecting stranger and boldly announce "I wrote that book. You're currently staring at the author"?

Sad I know.

But what would you do if you were me?

OK I admit it.

I have done precisely that.

Some people seem genuinely pleased – if a little surprised.

Some, however, beat a hasty retreat, checking I've not been using some elaborate distraction technique to pick their pockets.

One person was so thrilled he asked me to wait until he had bought a copy and then got me to sign it.

I am not sure it was quite my 15 minutes of fame, but it certainly lasted 15 seconds.

Thankfully no one has called me "saddo".

Not yet anyway.

However, even more exciting than this, is when people contact me to tell me how the book has helped them.

And literally hundreds of people have.

Why?

Well clearly I would like it to be down purely to the fact that people felt compelled to do so.

And in several cases that would be correct.

However, the overwhelming majority of people contacted me because they took up my challenge in the chapter "How to be your own best mate", particularly the section "Perform plastic surgery on your mind". I hope you also take up the challenge as well. But be patient – you'll come to it later.

It has also been fascinating to see the wide range of people who have benefited from the book. From students to sports stars it seems we could all benefit from an increase in self-confidence.

As for this 2nd edition, as well as adding to certain sections of the book I have also included a brand new chapter on "How to handle conflict confidently". Conflict is an inevitable part of life. That is not a note of defeatism but reality. But conflict, when handled well, can lead to creative solutions and improved performance and results.

Unresolved conflict can't.

So rather than avoid it at all costs this new chapter aims to give you the confidence to welcome it when appropriate and deal with it constructively and with increased confidence. Also in this 2nd edition I've added even more strategies and exercises to the chapter "How to be your own best mate", provoked partly by a phrase I heard on television: "We write our successes in sand but our setbacks in stone". Having recently worked with a group of people who were about to be made redundant I was both bemused and saddened by their inability to indentify and talk about their strengths with any confidence. Clearly it seems we can take our strengths for granted, so you'll find some advice and insights to help you take an honest and positive look at yourself without becoming arrogant. Having recently road-tested this material I know you're going to find this of real benefit.

One person who spent his life helping people to build their confidence and pursue their dreams was my good friend Clive Gott. In the 1st edition Clive was one of the people I publicly thanked for their support over the years. In the chapter "You'll get by with a little help from your friends", Clive was one of those rare people who fulfilled all four roles discussed in this section.

Clive sadly passed away in February 2011.

I miss him.

He was aged 52.

My last chapter is called "Have you got the confidence to go M.A.D?" M.A.D. simply stands for "Making A Difference". Like all of us Clive had his moments of self-doubt.

He didn't try to hide them – at times he wore them on his sleeve in a very open and public way. But he was M.A.D. He made a difference. And his confidence and self-belief was and still is an inspiration to me. Not because he was confident, but because of what his confidence led him to accomplish. As an adventurer he climbed many actual mountains, but his stories and wisdom helped many others climb their own "personal mountains".

Clive's death has been a painful reminder of how short my time on this planet can be. I want to make the most of the journey.

Do you?

If so then I hope the following pages bring you both the information and perhaps more importantly the inspiration to make the most of your life. If a lack of self-confidence is currently holding you back I hope what you read will propel you forward to a better future.

I've realized that life is at times a rollercoaster. I have never been so acutely aware of that fact than I am now. So I'm grateful I have had people like Clive with me to share at least some of the ride. I hope you have people like Clive in your life too. Perhaps the following pages will help you to discover who they are.

And maybe as a result of what you're about to read you will feel even better equipped to help others on their journey as well.

I'm aware we probably won't get the opportunity to meet face to face, but I do see it as a privilege that you have invested your time and perhaps even your money (well, I guess you could have borrowed it) to read this book.

So far countless people feel it's been a worthwhile investment.

I hope you do too.

Look for the nuggets.

Ignore the stuff that's not relevant.

And challenge what you don't agree with.

But above all do something with it.

For your sake.

And perhaps for the sake of others also.

And if you want to keep up to date with my thoughts on this subject, and a variety of others, then please follow me on Twitter: @TheSumoGuy.

Thanks.

Paul McGee
The SUMO Guy

Introduction

"It's all about confidence."
Eric Cantona

Cast your mind back to when you were growing up.

Do you remember getting injections from the doctor or school nurse when you were a kid?

Well, imagine if one of those jabs was to make you immune to the negative impact of rejection, failure and a lack of self-belief.

In other words, you were given an injection of confidence.

What would your life be like if you'd always felt confident?

What would it be like if you could get your confidence booster jab every five years?

What would you do? Where would you go? What would you attempt?

It's an interesting thought.

Agree?

For a start, you'd certainly have no need for this book.

Life could be so much more simple and straightforward.

But it's not.

Life is complex.

And your confidence can be fragile.

It can take years to grow and develop

and yet

one single event can crush it.

So why is confidence so crucial to you and your success and fulfilment in life?

What or who determines your level of confidence?

What happens when your confidence has been crushed?

Can it be rebuilt?

And if so, how?

How can you call on your confidence when you want to be at your best?

That's what this book is about.

In many ways, it's about creating a few more Kevins.

Let me explain.

I was wrapping up a two-day workshop for a group of redundant coal miners on "How to get that job". The event had gone well.

"So what's been the main benefit of the course?" I asked the 12 or so men gathered in the room. I was met with the usual replies that I'd heard countless times before.

"I feel a lot more positive about the future."

"I know how to sell myself more."

"I'll be better prepared for interviews."

Then it came to Kevin's turn.

"If you'd been my teacher at school, Paul, I could have been an astronaut."

I hadn't expected that answer.

Kevin went on. "Since I've been a kid my life has been mapped out for me. My Dad worked in a mine and it was just expected that I would follow.

I feel this course has given me a lot more belief in myself. I just wish I'd been on it 20 years ago. Who knows where I might be today if I had?"

I've never forgotten Kevin's words.

They're a reminder of how self-belief, or the lack of it, can influence the rest of our lives. I don't want a lack of confidence to cause me to look back on my life and reflect: "I wish I had."

I want to be the kind of person who says: "I'm glad I did."

I want to be a player, not a spectator.

What about you?

Getting More from Your Read

Let me explain my approach to writing this book. I've divided it into two sections.

Section One focuses on gaining more of an understanding about confidence. I explore why it's so fundamentally important to every aspect of our lives. I also expose some of the myths around confidence and uncover some of the half-baked ideas on the subject that actually do more harm than good. I end this first section by examining how our past affects who we are today and how we think and feel about ourselves.

Section Two focuses entirely on practical ways and ideas to help boost, build and develop your confidence. Whether you're struggling with self-doubt, been made redundant, recovering from a broken relationship or about to go on a date, there are dozens of practical and ready-to-apply tips and ideas to help you move on to fulfill your potential.

Style: I've deliberately written this book so that it's easy on the eye. I find long paragraphs and large blocks of text daunting, so I hope I've made it easier for you to absorb and retain the information.

Pit Stop

Pit Stops: You will also notice sections called Pit Stops. These are vital to your ability to get the most from this book.

After all, what's your goal here? To finish reading a book or to grow and develop your confidence?

If it's the latter – which I sincerely hope it is – then you will find the Pit Stops invaluable.

You see, I don't simply want you to read this book. I want you to engage with it. That means taking time out to reflect on and answer the Pit Stop questions.

You'll gain so much more from this book when you do. Promise.

The Personal Stuff

Personal Stuff: In order to add colour and context to the ideas I explore, I've also included sections called "Personal Stuff". These are examples of situations that I and others have experienced and that help reinforce and illustrate points in the book. Stories are a great way to engage in the learning process, and I hope that by providing a window into my world you will find things that you can relate to and identify with.

If the Personal Stuff doesn't tick your box that's fine. I believe they'll provide a richer experience for you, but they aren't essential to the text. You will still discover a load of tools to equip and enable yourself and others to grow in self-belief and overcome self-doubt if you decide simply to skip through the stories. But I hope you don't.

Finally, I'm aware that this book will probably find a home within the self-help genre. Some of those books are a little too sugar-coated for my taste, and perhaps for yours as well. Therefore you'll find my approach very down to earth, practical and, above all, realistic.

And please be aware that I'm not here to be nice. I'm here to be helpful.

So be prepared to be challenged as well as equipped to deal with the roller-coaster experience of life. My aim is to provide you with the ideas and inspiration to do so while hopefully raising the occasional smile along the way.

Finally, I really do believe that Eric Cantona was on to something when he said: "It's all about confidence." So wherever you are on your journey at the moment, I genuinely hope that this book provides you with the confidence to make a difference.

Enjoy.

Paul McGee – The SUMO Guy.

SECTION ONE

The Stuff You Need to Know

1 Why Self-Confidence is the X-Factor for Life

You're about to discover

The long-
term impact
confidence can
have on your life.

Why a small change can
make a big difference.

Why everyone benefits from an
increase in self-confidence.

The real upsides of increasing your
self-confidence.

What's the Big Deal about Confidence?

If you were to meet the film actor Tom Cruise, there are probably several things you would notice about him:

His smile.

His eyes.

And probably his height.

He's 5 feet 7 inches (or 170 cm). Some people regard that as being a little on the small side. In some cultures Tom's height would make him below average in height for a man.

Now imagine this. What if Tom Cruise increased his height by 10 percent? Not a huge amount is it?

So what's the outcome?

Well, suddenly Tom goes from being 5 foot 7 inches to being over 6 feet 1 inch (185 cm). He goes from below average height to above average height. He goes from being seen as small to being seen as tall.

And how much did he increase his height by?

10 percent. That's all.

A small change can make a big difference.

The bad news for Tom is that although he can try and appear to be taller than he actually is, the truth is there's not really a lot he can do about his height.

But as you may have gathered, this isn't a book about how tall you are, it's about increasing your self-confidence. And whereas there's not much you can do about your height, there's plenty you can do to increase your confidence.

What happens if you ignore all the advice in this book? What if you don't take steps to increase your self-confidence? Is it really such a big deal?

Well actually, yes.

As you're about to find out.

Imagine the scene. You're reading a job advert. It sounds like a great opportunity. You're ideally suited to the job. Well, almost. There's one area of experience that you lack. You focus on this one area.

Then the internal chatter begins.

"There'll clearly be others who apply who are more suitable than me. If only I had more experience. Mind you, I'd hate to be at an interview and get exposed due to my lack of knowledge. Anyway, there'll be hundreds of applicants and my CV is out of date. I'll leave it for now."

Imagine the scene. Your boss is keen for either you or your colleague to make a short presentation at the annual company conference. It's being held in Paris this year and it would be a brilliant opportunity to make a name for yourself and raise your profile within the company.

Then the internal chatter begins.

"I hate making presentations. All those people looking at me. I'd be awful with my nerves. What would I say? I don't want to look like a fool in front of all my colleagues – I'd never live down the embarrassment. Sam's really good at presentations, nothing seems to faze her. I guess she'll be the one that gets all the glory. Never mind, these conferences are always a good laugh – and they usually have a free bar on the last night."

Imagine the scene. You're at the pub. You and a group of mates have hooked up with a few friends you knew from college. Lisa catches your eye. You've always liked her, but it's been a while since you last saw each other. There's a definite attraction. Lisa looks in your direction and smiles.

Then the internal chatter begins.

"She's way out of my league. She used to go out with Martin. Why would she be interested in me? OK, so she's smiling at me. She's probably just being friendly. I bet she feels sorry for me. I couldn't ask her out. No way. What if she turned me down? I'd never hear the last of it from my mates. Think I'll leave it this time."

So you don't apply for the job. You don't make the presentation. You don't ask the person out on a date.

Has your world ended? No. Are you a failure? No. Will it now be impossible to live a fulfilled life? No.

But be honest. Would a little more self-confidence have helped? I'm not talking about arrogance, brashness or becoming a raving extrovert. I'm talking about confidence. That sense of being OK about yourself. That awareness that it's OK to fail. That understanding that rejection doesn't mean the end of the world.

The truth is ...

> We could all benefit from a small increase in self-confidence.

A 10 percent increase could make all the difference.

It means you might have gone for the job. It means you might have made the presentation. It means you might have embarked on a romantic relationship.

You Don't Have to Be Ill

As I'm fond of saying, "You don't have to be ill to get better." You see, I'm not suggesting you have major problems with self-confidence. Nor am I suggesting that you're paranoid about speaking in public or taking risks. You may in fact be fairly happy and content in life.

But maybe there's more. More to do. More to become.

And what might be stopping you? Not enough self-belief and confidence?

That's where a small increase could make all the difference. Not an extreme personality makeover. A small change. That's all.

Let me put it another way. Have a look at the following diagram.

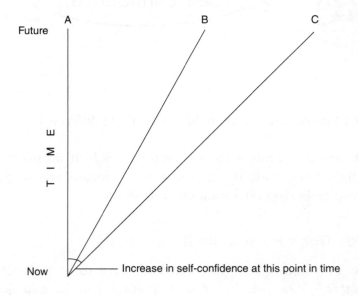

As the diagram illustrates, a small increase in your self-confidence will, *over time*, make a big difference to where you are in life (B). A further small change and *over time* you will find yourself in a significantly different place (C) from where you might otherwise have been (A).

Your original destination (A) may still be a great place to be, but small changes today can take you further in your journey. B and C could represent activities and opportunities that you never dreamt were possible, but they demonstrate how a small change now can literally transform your future.

Let me put it another way.

You're on a ship heading from the UK to New York. But when the ship sets sail it's just a few degrees off course. If it remains off course you end up somewhere in the Caribbean. That's approximately 1,500 miles from New York.

A small change in direction (or confidence) can lead to a completely different destination.

Pit Stop

∞ What could be happening in your life if you were at point B or point C?
∞ Write down three benefits to you if your confidence could increase by 10 percent.
∞ Imagine one activity or scenario that would happen if you had more confidence.
∞ Imagine how you'd feel if you didn't make any attempt to increase your confidence.

It's like most things in life, they add up. Let's say you currently weigh 75 kg and over the next ten years you increase your weight by 2 kg a year. At first you would hardly notice the small increase in weight. But over time you and other people would notice. It might happen gradually and you can adjust your clothes accordingly – but the bottom line is that in ten years' time you would be 20 kg heavier. Your life and your health could be radically different from where you are now.

A small increase makes a big difference.

Here's another illustration.

Ever make your own bread? As I've found to my cost, the bread won't rise without yeast.

You only need a small amount of yeast, but without it you've got flat bread.

That's how our lives can be without confidence. We fail to rise. We fail to achieve our potential.

I'll say it again. A small change over time makes a big difference.

This book is about how you can make those small changes to your life and enjoy the benefits of doing so.

The Personal Stuff

"Never forget that the world's your oyster." It was a message my mum used to drum into me as a child. To be fair, interrupting me while I was watching *The Magic Roundabout* was overdoing it at times – but she meant well.

What motivated her to keep on repeating this message? Well, I'm not sure my mum had a great deal of self-confidence. Neither did she get a lot of encouragement in her own childhood but I sense that she was determined that her lack should not be my legacy.

From an early age she spotted that I had a talent for and an interest in acting and telling stories. She did all she could to encourage me. She made it clear that waiting around for things to happen wasn't a great recipe for success. If you want something, go out and get it.

But as you'll see later in this book, I still grew up with feelings of inadequacy and insecurity. I was plagued by a swarm of self-doubt in relation to my appearance, my weight and my poor manual dexterity.

However, in one particular area of life I felt good. I felt confident. In fact, I felt very confident. That was speaking in front of people.

I had an ability in this area and, more importantly, I had the encouragement to use and develop it. And when ability meets encouragement, you've got a pretty potent weapon.

Wouldn't you agree?

Nevertheless, talent didn't dramatically manifest itself one day. It grew over time.

It started with school plays. First as a shepherd, but then as Buttons in the school Christmas production of Cinderella (it was one of the leading roles, I promise you). It's influenced my whole life ever since, as the following story illustrates.

I was having coffee with Sue. She worked for a TV company. Halfway through my caffè latte she took a phone call. I surveyed the sights and sounds of Manchester and sought to feign a complete lack of interest in Sue's less than private telephone conversation.

The call ended and Sue brought me up to speed.

"That's a guy I know who works on the *Question Time* TV programme with David Dimbleby. The bloke they normally use as the audience warm-up man has gone off sick. They need a replacement. I'll have to ring Ted and see if he's available."

Ted was not available. They had a problem.

She looked at me. "Do you fancy doing it, Paul?"

"What, me?" I asked, summoning up all my powers to appear humble and rather nonchalant about her request. "But Sue, I'm not a stand-up comedian. I've never been a warm-up man before."

To be honest, it wasn't a genuine objection but more a desire to gain some reassurance from Sue. It worked.

"You don't need to be a comedian. It's a *Question Time* audience. They just need a little bit of er ... em. ... warming up, I guess. Just tell a few stories, get them laughing a little and think of something that involves them talking to each other."

That's all I had to hear. I didn't need any further convincing. I felt confident in my abilities to do a good job.

I even had an idea for an ice-breaker. I'd split the audience into pairs and get them discussing the following: If a Martian came down from Mars (which is presumably where they're from) and asked you to give a definition of the word "politician", what would your answer be?

Once they replied I could give them my answer:

Politician comes from the word "politics", which can be broken down as follows:

Poli meaning many
Tics meaning blood-sucking parasites.

The next evening I was indeed the warm-up man for the *Question Time* programme. It went really well. The audience loved my definition of politics. I had the opportunity to meet, talk, work and then later enjoy dinner with David Dimbleby. It was a great evening.

But it was an evening that wouldn't have happened if I hadn't had the confidence to say "yes".

I know what you're thinking: "You were lucky. You were having coffee with Sue when she took the call."

You're right, I was. But I don't see that as luck – I see it as an opportunity. An opportunity that I could always have decided to say no to. But I didn't.

The fact is that the world is **your** oyster. The little kid who started off life playing a shepherd in a school play could always end up working with the BBC.

Pit Stop

∞ Have you ever had an opportunity that you really wanted to take but you said no rather than yes?
∞ What stopped you saying yes?
∞ Imagine you had taken the opportunity and it had turned out really well. What would the benefits to you have been?

Self-Confidence is the Key

As the previous story illustrates, having an opportunity helps. Having ability was pretty important as well.

But ultimately, the key was having the self-confidence to say "yes". It was having the confidence and belief in my own abilities and potential, even though I had never done that work before.

So did that experience change my life? No, it didn't. But it certainly enhanced it. By saying yes, I proved to myself what I was capable of doing. It gave me the self-belief to seize other opportunities. I grew in confidence. And I promise you, there will be times when having the self-confidence to take action and seize the opportunity _will_ change your life.

The truth is ...

A small change can make a really big difference.

Self-Confidence – What it will and won't lead to

It won't lead to you

∞ Being transformed into Superman or Wonder Woman.
∞ Floating through life from one success to another.
∞ Being immune to setbacks and challenges.
∞ Never having to feel disappointed, despondent or dejected.
∞ Taking unnecessary and uncalculated risks.
∞ Feeling you must have all the answers.
∞ Feeling you always have to be an extrovert when deep down you're an introvert.

It will put you in a better position to

∞ Attempt new things and discover new places.
∞ Discover talents you never knew you had.
∞ Seize new opportunities.

- ∞ Become a more enjoyable person to be around.
- ∞ Feel better about yourself.
- ∞ Fulfill your potential and discover your purpose in life.
- ∞ Make a positive difference in the lives of others.

- ∞ Which of the above benefits of increased self-confidence are most important to you right now? (Tick your top three.)
- ∞ Why did you pick those particular ones?
- ∞ What are the consequences for you personally if you don't grow in confidence?

How Confidence can Help You Make the Most of Life

I first used the next illustration in my SUMO book, but it's worth revisiting. Imagine seven people lined up in a row.

Now imagine that each person represents a day of the week.

Monday   Tuesday   Wednesday   Thursday   Friday   Saturday   Sunday

Now for the potentially scary part. Imagine that each day of the week represents a decade of your life.

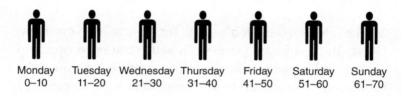

| Monday | Tuesday | Wednesday | Thursday | Friday | Saturday | Sunday |
| 0–10 | 11–20 | 21–30 | 31–40 | 41–50 | 51–60 | 61–70 |

So which day of the week are you on in your life? At the time of writing I'm on Friday lunchtime. I've still got the weekend to look forward to, and I'm hoping to add a couple of extra days to my week by having a bank holiday Monday and Tuesday!

It puts things into perspective, doesn't it?

The challenge is to make the most of your journey, what-ever day you're on. What that journey looks like and what experiences it involves will be influenced by lots of factors – particularly your level of confidence.

Pit Stop

- ∞ Which day of the week are you on? How does that make you feel?
- ∞ How determined are you to make the most of the rest of your journey?
- ∞ What has a lack of self-confidence prevented you from achieving so far?
- ∞ Look out for ideas in this book to enhance your journey and use them to help others as well.

It's Time for Some Honesty

Let's turn the spotlight onto you.

Maybe life is going fairly well for you at the moment. Great. But could an increase in self-confidence open up opportunities you're not even aware of yet? A new job? Promotion? New business? New home? New partner? (Although I'm not suggesting there's anything wrong with your current one if you have one.)

Could a good life become a great one?

On the other hand, maybe life isn't going well for you at present. Maybe it's become a bit of a struggle. Perhaps your life feels a bit like a game of snakes and ladders – except there's a distinct lack of ladders on the board.

If that's the case, self-confidence will be crucial to your recovery.

But where do you find it? Where are the ladders? What snakes have led you to the position you're in now?

Read on, because whether your self-confidence seems relatively good or is in need of a major boost, you're about to discover plenty of answers.

Unfortunately though, not all the answers and ideas for developing your self-confidence are particularly helpful – as you're about to discover.

in A Nutshell

∞ Everyone can benefit from an increase in self-confidence – you don't have to be ill to get better.

∞ Focus on the 10 percent difference – over time it makes a big impact.

∞ Increasing your self-confidence doesn't guarantee an easy ride in life, but it will improve the quality of the journey.

2 Taking the "Con" Out of Confidence

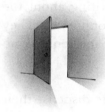

You're about to discover

The five big
myths about
confidence and
how to debunk them.

Myth number one: Once
you have confidence you can
master anything.

Myth number two: Some people are just
born confident.

Myth number three: Humility is the
opposite of confidence.

Myth number four: There can be no
room for self-doubt.

Myth number five: Alcohol gives
you confidence.

Five Myths around Developing Self-Confidence

The world of self-help has grown massively in the last 20 years. It's a multibillion-dollar industry. There are some brilliant books available that I believe can have a profound effect on helping you make the most of life. But there's also a lot of crap out there.

You will find plenty of so-called gurus writing about the effortless way to achieve success or gain confidence. They give the impression that everything is easy and requires no effort. I disagree.

The truth is that a lot of people are happy to dispense their quick-fix solutions to complex problems. And it's easy to be seduced by their false promises. It's also easy to become disillusioned very quickly.

Here are a few myths we need to debunk as we aim to take the con out of confidence.

Myth Number One: Once You Have Confidence You can Master Anything

I wish this were true, but it's not. I'm a fairly confident person, but no matter how confident I become, I will never be able to run the 100 metres in under 10 seconds, sing like Pavarotti or bend a ball like David Beckham.

You see, confidence is crucial to our success, but so too is competence.

Let me explain.

Confidence without Competence = Delusion

To see examples of this, watch the early rounds of a reality music talent show on television. They're overflowing with talentless, self-deluded people with shedloads of confidence. But confidence is not enough. We also need ability.

Sadly, there's also the flipside.

Competence without Confidence = Unfulfilled Potential

This scenario is a real tragedy: people who possess the capability but lack the self-belief to use it.

To illustrate this further, the confidence and competence matrix may help.

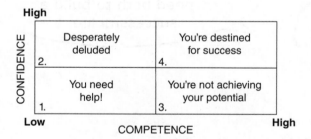

1   Low competence and low confidence = You need help!
2   Low competence and high confidence = You're desperately deluded.

3   High competence and low confidence = You're not achieving your potential.

4   High competence and high confidence = You're destined for success.

Confidence can be crucial to success, but it's not the only key to achieving it. You also need to develop competence. Self-confidence might spur you on to seek help and support from others, but ultimately it's developing your skills and learning from experience that will cement your success.

And that takes **time** and **effort** – no matter what other gurus tell you.

The truth is …

> If competence is the bricks then confidence is the mortar. And you need both to build a successful life.

Myth Number Two: Some People are Just Born Confident

There is a certain amount of truth in this statement. On a very basic level, some children are born more towards the extrovert end of the spectrum, while others are more towards the introvert.

However, being an extrovert doesn't equate to you automatically being confident. You may be predisposed to being more socially confident and comfortable around people, but as we'll see in the next chapter, it's also quite easy to have your confidence crushed by others.

Equally, a more introverted person may feel less comfortable being around people than an extrovert, but that doesn't mean that with the right encouragement, opportunity and environment, they won't grow in confidence.

Here's the bottom line: Whatever our predisposition and personality type when we're born, everyone has the capability to increase their self-confidence.

The truth is ...

There is no confidence gene. It's not a case of either you've got it or you haven't.

The "you are born confident" myth also fails to take into account the following factors.

Confidence is situational

If I had to rate myself on a scale of 1–10 in terms of how confident I felt in any given situation – 1 = Low/uncomfortable, 10 = High/very confident – my ratings would vary and my list would look something like this. Rate yourself as well, and see how you compare with my scores.

Situation	My score	Your score
Cooking a meal for friends	6	
Changing a wheel on my car	4	
Writing an article on my chosen subject	8	
Speaking French when visiting France	3	
Delivering a motivational talk to 6,000 people	9.5	
Erecting some flat-packed furniture	0.5	
Talking to a group of strangers	9	
Resolving a technical issue on my PC	0	
Making a complaint in a hotel or restaurant	9	

Plot those results on a chart and it would look something like this.

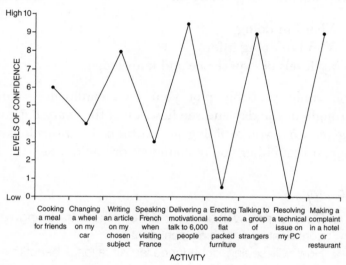

Some people perceive me as confident because they see me in a work setting (where in all humility I believe I'm highly competent) or in a social gathering (where due to my personality and previous experience I do feel generally very comfortable).

My mum always encouraged me to engage with adults when I was a child. My job demands that I meet and greet delegates when they arrive at events. As I attempt to make them feel at ease, it also has the same effect on me.

In other words, I've grown in confidence – I wasn't born that way.

The same goes for you.

You will notice from the above list that my confidence levels fluctuate depending on:

∞ What I'm doing
∞ Who I'm doing it for
∞ My levels of experience and knowledge

You could probably plot your own confidence scores throughout the day and see how much they vary depending on what you're doing at the time. It's ridiculous to suggest that either you're confident or you're not.

Pit Stop

∞ Do you simply label yourself or others as being confident or not being confident?
∞ How will seeing confidence as situational benefit you?
∞ Write down something you need to develop your competence in so that your confidence will grow in that area.

Myth Number Three: Humility is the Opposite of Confidence

A retired Premiership football referee happily confessed on radio that even if a referee makes a mistake they should never admit to it. His reasoning? People won't have confidence in you if you admit you got something wrong. To own up to a mistake would be a sign of weakness.

What utter garbage.

The phrase "being confident means never admitting your mistakes" belongs in the same dustbin as "love means never having to say you're sorry".

You see, there's a fine line between self-confidence and arrogance. And when you think maintaining your confidence means you can't admit to making mistakes, you've just crossed it.

In my book, humility is not about appearing weak, putting yourself down or allowing people to walk all over you. Humility is about having a healthy regard for yourself. It's about being confident and secure in the knowledge that it's OK to make mistakes – and not being arrogant enough to believe that you'll never make any. It's having the confidence to admit that there are some areas in life where you may have very little confidence in your ability at the moment (erecting flat-packed furniture springs to mind for me), but you're not going to beat yourself up over it.

Humility and self-confidence may seem like an unlikely marriage, but they actually make a great couple.

The fact is in certain areas of your life you won't grow in confidence until you have the humility to recognize that you need the help of others.

However, sometimes your search for help doesn't always provide you with the answers you're looking for. There are a few whacky ideas on how to increase your confidence, as you're about to discover.

Self-Confidence

The Personal Stuff

I guess it all started with Derek. In the annals of history there were no MP3s, iPods or CDs, there were audio cassette tapes.

Derek, my ex-boss from Dudley, suggested that I listen to some tapes by a British guy called Richard Denny. He was a motivational speaker and his area of specialism was "sales".

I don't remember much of what he said, but there was one phrase he used. I've never forgotten it.

"Within every adversity, there is a seed of equal or greater opportunity."

I had just lost my job. I needed inspiration. I needed hope. That quote gave me some.

It started me on a journey into the sometimes slightly strange and occasionally whacky world of self-help and personal development. If I'm honest, it triggered an obsession.

Some people follow their football team home and away. Others stand on deserted railway platforms or buy shoes by the truckload. Not me. My passion was personal development – and I was hooked, big time.

I listened to a lot of American speakers. I read their books. I even went on to attend their live seminars in far-flung places such as Yorkshire. In fact, I heard so many American speakers I even began to sound and act like one.

It was bizarre. I started doing high-fives – with myself. I chewed gum and when I went shopping I said "Have a nice day" to the 17-year-old check-out girl at the supermarket. (However, I drew the line at having my teeth whitened and walking around with a permanent grin.)

Still, I found the material incredibly helpful. And when you have no job, a mystery illness and are living on invalidity benefit, you're glad of any help you can get.

I listened to a tape by a guy called Randy from California. For some reason, despite the passing of time, his name has always stuck with me. He spoke about building self-esteem and confidence. Without them, he argued, we are doomed to live a life of misery and unfulfilled potential. (I'm a Bradford City supporter, so his words seemed particularly pertinent.)

Randy spoke a lot about the negative impact of low self-esteem and confidence, not just for ourselves but for society as a whole. But there was an answer. There was a way to claim back what was rightfully ours. There was a way to awaken the sleeping giant within each and every one of us.

I sat alone in my kitchen, completely engrossed by his message. My heightened state of excitement and antici-pation raised my body temperature. I removed my anorak.

And then Randy delivered his life-changing strategy. It involved ...

Wait for it ...

Standing naked in front of a mirror.

What people listening to Randy as they drove to work thought of this, I'm not sure. Perhaps some, desperate that their life of unfulfilled potential should not last a second longer, pulled over to the side of the road and began undressing. If questioned by the police they could always rewind the tape: "Listen to this for yourself, officer. Randy's a motivational speaker from California. I'm raising my self-esteem as we speak."

But Randy didn't want us just to stand naked. He wanted us to affirm every part of our body by touching it and saying:

I affirm these ankles, I accept them I value them.

I affirm these knees, I accept them I value them.

I affirm these thighs, I accept them I value them.

I affirm these testi …

I think you get Randy's point.

As I sat alone in the kitchen with only my Madonna wall calendar for company, small pockets of Mancunian cynicism bubbled to the surface. Stand naked in front of a mirror? Affirm every part of my body whilst touching it? I wanted to build my confidence, not join a cult.

I was humble enough to realize I needed help, but I hadn't quite reached enough of a desperation point that I'd try anything.

Pit Stop

∞ Come up with your own definition of humility. Humility is …

∞ How easy do you find it asking others for help?

∞ Have you ever come across whacky advice on how to boost your confidence? If so, what was it?

Myth Number Four: There can be No Room for Self-Doubt

Being wracked with self-doubt isn't a great recipe for success. But, perhaps surprisingly, it's both healthy and helpful to have a small degree of self-doubt.

It prevents complacency. It can motivate you to improve and to want to get better. In fact, it's quite normal to have a degree of self-doubt – it's what makes us human. (The exception to the above I guess could be in a sporting event at a crucial stage of the game. Acknowledging or allowing even a small degree of self-doubt to enter your thinking when you're about to serve for the match, take a penalty or kick for goal could be debilitating.)

You'd be surprised how seemingly successful and out-wardly confident people still wrestle with self-doubt, as the following story reveals.

The Personal Stuff

I've recently finished reading a fascinating book by the British comedian Frank Skinner. I guess if you make a living standing in front of hundreds, and in Frank's case thousands, of people trying to make them laugh, it's only natural to assume that there can be no room for self-doubt. Right?

Wrong.

In his book, *Frank Skinner on the Road* (published by Century), he talks about a review of a show that read: "Frank Skinner is, to all intents and purposes, a comedy God."

What does Frank focus on? The phrase "comedy God"? No, he focuses on the words "to all intents and purposes". He wrestles with what those words actually mean and whether indeed the review is as positive as it first seems. In fact, because of such mental gymnastics Frank does his upmost to avoid reading any reviews of his work.

In a way far better than I could ever express, he goes on to write about his relationship with self-doubt:

> *Doubt is my constant sidekick. I doubt my work, my faith, my relationships. If you're a human being, doubt comes with the job, doesn't it? When Jesus was dying on the cross, he suddenly looks up and shouts "My God, my God, why hast thou forsaken me?" Even Jesus! And then he dies. He couldn't die until he'd become wholly human; and he couldn't be wholly human until he'd experienced doubt.*

This may be one of the most important "secrets" about self-confidence: a certain degree of doubt is both normal and natural.

When you next see someone who appears to be "together", relaxed and super-confident (like a stand-up comedian in front of several thousand people), remember beneath that façade is a human being who might well be wrestling with the same inadequacies and insecurities as you are.

However

this next point is crucial.

That person still has enough self-confidence not to allow their insecurities to rob them of the opportunity to achieve success and fulfill their potential.

The truth is ...

Self-confidence is not the absence of self-doubt. It's being able to live with your doubt as your companion but not as your master.

Myth Number Five: Alcohol Gives You Confidence

Richard and I were out for a drink recently.

"What are you having, mate?" I asked.

"I'll have a pint of Courage please Paul."

If only it were that easy, I thought – being able to order courage or confidence by the pint.

But alcohol is the route to confidence for some people. It often goes by the name of Dutch courage. One glass may take the edge off their nerves, but some people don't stop at one drink. Before they know it they're feeling extremely confident in themselves.

That's the problem when the only source of your confidence is alcohol. You overestimate your own abilities and you underestimate the potential negative consequences of your actions. Alcohol-fuelled confidence has conned you into a false sense of security and of your own infallibility and immortality.

Let's acknowledge the pleasure that alcohol can bring but also the pain. In terms of developing confidence, it's a quick-fix solution with some potentially negative long-term consequences.

in A Nutshell

When you're growing in self-confidence you need to remember:

∞ Mastering confidence doesn't mean you can master anything – it's linked to competence and will fluctuate depending on your ability and the context of your situation.

∞ There is no confidence gene – you're not born confident. No matter where you start from, everyone can grow in confidence.

∞ Humility is not the opposite of self-confidence. They're an unlikely but necessary partnership.

∞ There *can* be room for self-doubt in the midst of self-confidence. Just remember not to let it become your master.
∞ The positive effects of alcohol are temporary, but the negative effects could last a lifetime.
∞ You don't have to dance naked to grow in confidence (unless you really want to, that is).

So Far

∞ We've explored why self-confidence is a big deal.
∞ We've debunked some modern myths around confidence.

Now we're going to take time to reflect on what – or perhaps more accurately *who* – has influenced your current level of self-confidence.

3 Who Crushed Your Confidence? Your Upbringing

You're about to discover

Why looking
back can help
you move forward.

How your beliefs affect
your confidence.

The impact of your upbringing on
what you think about yourself.

Why some people are "Awfulisers" and
how to deal with them.

Having worked as both a counsellor and a performance coach, I'm convinced that if we want to understand ourselves and why we sometimes lack confidence, then we must be prepared to revisit some potentially challenging previous experiences.

Doing so could make us feel a little uncomfortable but let me explain why it's so important that we do.

We all have a story. We all have a history, a set of experiences from the past that shape and influence who we are today.

For you, it may have been a relatively pleasant journey so far. Your story is full of positive memories, with only the occasional blip. For others, the journey has resembled a roller-coaster of highs and lows. And for some people, the journey so far (to use an earlier metaphor) has been a bit like playing a game of snakes and ladders – except without the ladders.

Maybe you had a difficult childhood.
Maybe you've failed an exam or screwed up at school.
Maybe you married young and lived to regret it.
Maybe you feel you've never done as well in life as your
    brother or sister.
Maybe you've been made redundant.
Maybe your partner walked out on you and the kids.
Maybe lots of things have happened to you that you wish
    had just never happened. But they have.

Put quite simply, you have a choice. These experiences can destroy your confidence, or they can awaken it. Your past can make you bitter or it can make you better.

So what's it to be?

The goal of this book is to help you move forward and grow in self-confidence. But before we move into first gear, we're going to go into reverse. We're going back in order to help us move forward.

And beware, there will be some navel-gazing along the way. When you navel-gaze you may discover some "navel fluff", which is another way of saying you may find some stuff from your past that you would prefer to ignore.

But, in order to understand where we are, it's useful to understand where we've come from and how we got here. When we do that, moving on becomes so much easier. In some ways it's a bit like an illness – once it's been diagnosed we're in a much better position to treat it. Likewise, once we've found the causes for our lack of confidence we can do something about it.

I'm not suggesting that we examine every aspect of our past and hold our parents or whoever up for derision because of some minor misdemeanour on their part. (If the misdemeanour was major, then you should probably seek some professional help.)

Neither is this a competition for who can navel-gaze the longest. Navel-gazing is necessary, but it's temporary. As a process it's more of a holiday fling, not a lifetime commitment.

Our goal is to learn from our past, not wallow in it. Acknowledge your pain if that's what you need to do, but you don't have to relive it in detail.

So are you ready? Seat belt fastened? Tray in the upright position?

Good. Because we're about to embark on the "Explain Game". It's a game that will provide plenty of clues and insights as to why you sometimes lack self-confidence. Once you have an understanding of the causes for your lack of confidence, you're in a better position to deal with them. Discovering an explanation puts you in a better position to find a solution rather than simply playing the role of victim. However, just make sure you avoid a similar-sounding but far more destructive pastime, the "Blame Game".

Let's start by looking at something that influences every aspect of our lives. We've all got them, but rarely do we take time to understand how we acquired them.

What am I talking about? Your beliefs.

How Beliefs Affect Your Confidence

What you believe about yourself, the world and other people can have a profound affect on your level of self-confidence. My friend Rob Whittaker says:

"If we believe a lie it might as well be the truth for the impact it has on us."

David Page once believed a lie. He didn't realize it was a lie at the time – he believed it was the truth. Let me explain.

I came across his story in the national papers. While digging in his yard, he picked up what looked like a classic example of a Second World War mine. In that split second before he realized the danger, he pressed the button on the top. Fearing that releasing the button would cause the bomb to detonate, he carried it to a shed and awkwardly strapped masking tape to his thumb to secure it firmly.

He then called 999. Sobbing on the phone, he told the woman police operator, "Tell my family I love them, if the worst comes to the worst." (He had a wife and five children.)

He was eventually put through to an Army expert on unexploded bombs, who confirmed that he should not take his thumb off the button under any circumstances.

Police, fire and ambulance officers arrived at the yard and a senior policeman (in rank, not age) helped David put his arm and the mine into a barrel of sand in order to lessen the likely damage if the bomb exploded.

Scary stuff, eh? Apparently it was four agonizing hours before the army bomb disposal squad arrived.

Four hours is a long time to wait. That guy must have been going through hell. Would he survive? If so, would he lose his arm?

His wife Jane supplied him with a hot water bottle and a blanket. I presume that was to keep him warm, as I doubt either item would be much use in an explosion.

When the army bomb disposal team arrived, they removed his arm from the barrel of sand and then the tape from his thumb.

Risky?

Not really.

Why?

Because they identified that what David Page was holding was not in fact an unexploded Second World War mine but part of a hydraulic system from an old Citroën car.

Recalling his ordeal, David Page said, "I was absolutely terrified that I would be blown into a million pieces – I was looking into the sky thinking my life was over."

To go back to Rob Whittaker's quote for a moment, "If we believe a lie, it might as well be the truth for the impact it has on us."

The truth is ...

> That's the thing about beliefs – they don't have to be true to be powerful.

Here's what's interesting about the word "beliefs". If you write it in a certain way, you suddenly realize something:

BE	LIE	FS

In other words, there can be a lie in the midst of your beliefs.

Sadly, some of the beliefs people have about themselves rob them of their confidence. Beliefs such as:

∞ Things always go wrong for me.
∞ I'm as thick as two short planks of wood.
∞ I'm ugly.
∞ I'll never do anything with my life.
∞ I can't change.
∞ I'll never be as good as ...
∞ My best years are behind me.

Maybe it's time to question the truth about such beliefs and expose them for what they really are – lies.

Pit Stop

- ∞ Which of the above statements could you identify with?
- ∞ What are the ramifications for you in having those beliefs?
- ∞ Who do you know who has some of these beliefs about themselves?
- ∞ What other beliefs do you have that could be having a negative effect on you?

Who Influences Your Beliefs about Yourself?

Lots of factors influence your beliefs about yourself. Here are four of them:

- ∞ Your upbringing
- ∞ Your school days
- ∞ The media
- ∞ Yourself

All four have the power to have a positive impact on us – but on the flipside, they also have the potential to crush or erode our confidence.

This chapter focuses on your upbringing. Section Two explores the impact of your time at school, the media and how you affect your own confidence.

To introduce the impact of your upbringing, let's go into some personal stuff.

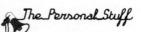

The Personal Stuff

This is Tony's story:

My mum remarried when I was eight years old. Her new husband, Jim, had never had children of his own. At first he seemed to like me. He had an interest in football and I guess looking back I thought that would be something we could do together. I loved playing football at school and when I told Jim how well I was doing, it seemed to meet with his approval. In fact, the better I said I played, the more approval I gained.

I think I probably exaggerated how well I was doing, but when you're desperate for some recognition, "bigging yourself up" seems perfectly acceptable.

But after the initial honeymoon period, things turned sour. Jim watched me play a couple of times. He wasn't impressed.

I'm not sure what other factors came into play, but two years down the line we were hardly speaking to each other. What few words he did say to me were confined solely to the mocking variety. If Jim's character were like a hot drink, it would best be described as a "large moccha with a double shot of cynicism".

By the age of ten I was acquiring a bit of puppy fat. I didn't see it as much of a problem to begin with – in fact, I probably wasn't even aware of it until Jim started calling me "the big fat nancy boy" in his mocking tone. In some ways I could understand his comments about my weight, but not the term "nancy boy". However, as I avoided fights at school and didn't especially enjoy climbing trees or getting covered in mud, I guess in his eyes I must have been one.

I owned a bike. I was desperate to ride it more often. But Jim said I couldn't ride it. By that, I don't mean that he didn't allow me to ride it – he just believed (on what evidence I'm not sure) that I was physically incapable of riding one. Maybe that fitted in with his definition of a nancy boy. Nevertheless, I insisted I could ride and wanted to prove it.

One day my mum and Jim agreed to watch me ride my bike up the road. After an initial shaky start, I gradually grew in confidence and began to ride without wobbling. At one stage I even took one hand off the handlebars to demonstrate my confidence. As I cycled back towards them I beamed with a sense of pride and satisfaction.

I expected to be greeted with approval. None came.

"You were hopeless," barked Jim. "You're not safe to be on the road."

Not wanting to cause a scene, Mum remained quiet. Although I couldn't explain it at the time, I think on reflection that, due to her overprotecting nature, she was quite happy for me not to ride a bike. Not out of spite, but out of a genuine desire for my safety.

I didn't ride my bike for four years. When my mates went for a bike ride I used to run behind them. By the time I was given permission to ride one it was too small for me.

Finally, I got myself another bike and within two weeks I had my first puncture. I'd never fixed a puncture before. I'd never been shown how to fix one.

My mum persuaded Jim to show me how. He was to teaching what cannibals are to vegetarianism. I don't actually remember him showing me what to do, but what remains permanently etched on my mind as he stood watching my attempts was his barrage of mocking diatribe: "pathetic", "hopeless", "the nancy boy can't do it". Whoever wrote "Sticks and stones may break my bones, but names will never hurt me" clearly hadn't met my stepfather.

And the consequences of my encounters with Jim?

To this day I'm sensitive about my weight. I've never been particularly practical – maybe with some encouragement I might have been, but I shy away from it now. It's taken me years to recover my sense of self-confidence and even now I dread it if my own son's bike has a puncture.

I'm 45 years old now. My mum divorced Jim. I've only mentioned a couple of episodes. There were many more. I sometimes think about tracking him down and telling him how his psychological abuse affected me.

It's painful to read Tony's story. It illustrates the effect of an event that happened when he was young and impressionable and that still has an impact on him today. His beliefs about himself, his levels of self-confidence about his appearance and his competence to carry out a practical task were all shaped by an episode from the past.

I know Tony well. We work in a similar industry. His self-confidence may have been crushed, but meeting him now, you would never know the anguish he suffered as a child. He's a brilliant example of how you can recover and rebuild your confidence. In the later chapters you'll discover how to do that.

How Your Upbringing Influences Your Beliefs and Your Self-Confidence

Tony's story illustrates the power and impact of parents, or in his case a step-parent.

I was reading about the upbringing of a successful British comedian. He described his father, who died when the comedian was 17, as intimidating and curt. He lamented that his dad was not around to see what he'd achieved, but then added, "I wonder if I would have been this successful if my dad had still been alive. Maybe I wouldn't have had the confidence."

Sad, eh?

I believe that the majority of what parents do for their children is done with good intentions. There are obviously a number of exceptions to that, but overall I'm confident that when Mum or Dad gets out of bed in the morning, they're not thinking, "How can I screw up my kid's life today?"

However, the truth is ...

Sometimes good intentions + ignorance = negative outcomes.

Despite well-meaning intentions, the baggage and negative beliefs that the members of your family carry with them can be automatically passed down to you. Let's find out more.

Was Your Mum an Awfuliser?

What is an Awfuliser? It's not a word you'll come across in the dictionary. In fact, I made it up. Here's how you'll recognize one.

Awfulisers have a habit of turning a minor setback into a drama or a crisis. They tend to be life's worriers. Their favourite phrase is "That's awful." They have an uncanny ability to escalate the seriousness of an issue and in doing so they can leave you feeling – and this is the key point – *less confident* and less able to deal with your challenges.

Working with an Awfuliser can be challenging. Being in a long-term relationship with one isn't exactly fun at times either. But what if one of your parents is one? What if the person who is perceived in most cultures as the care giver and nurturer – that is, your mum – suffers from these tendencies?

What is the impact on you?
How does it influence your view of the world?
How does it influence your beliefs about yourself and your levels of confidence?

By the way, I'm not specifically having a pop at mums, it's just that *in my experience* (and I haven't conducted any clinical research into the matter), mothers generally have more of a tendency to exhibit this behaviour than fathers. This might not be your experience, which is fine. But whoever that person was, if they were your main care provider, the impact will be the same.

Before I dig up any more naval fluff and before you reach for the phone to give your mum (or whoever) some feedback, remember the following:

First, we're playing the "Explain Game" right now. The box marked "Blame Game" needs to remain locked away in the cupboard.

Secondly, finding someone to blame from your past won't help you grow in self-confidence. It may simply serve as an excuse to justify why you're not confident.

Here's something else worth considering. Most parents who are Awfulisers are the product of their own Awfulising parents. They're simply passing down their own hand-me-downs, which in this case is their attitude to life.

But now for the good news. You're the one who can help break the cycle. You have the insight, self-awareness and knowledge to stop passing on these harmful hand-me-down mindsets.

Pit Stop

∞ Who in your family has a tendency to be an
   Awfuliser?
∞ How did and does that affect you?
∞ Who in your family is the antidote to the Awfuliser?
   Who has given you positive beliefs about
   yourself?

What Motivates an Awfuliser?

We need to understand that an Awfuliser's biggest fault is
born out of good intentions. And their fault is?

They care.

Too much.

They over-care. They over-protect.

If they were a bird, all their chicks would be late develop-
ers. They'd struggle to have the heart to push their chicks
out of the nest so that they could learn to fly, even though
that's what birds are made to do.

As people, we're designed to grow, explore, take risks,
learn, make mistakes, experience the joy of victory and the
pain of defeat. But sometimes our growth is stunted and
our progress stifled by the well-meaning but ultimately
harmful over-protection of our mothers, fathers or people
who care for us.

When an Awfuliser over-protects they are in fact neglecting their children's natural desire to grow and explore. They can end up with an 18-year-old adult with the self-confidence of a 10-year-old child.

However, let's get one thing straight. There are much worse things a parent can do to their children.

I'm also not suggesting a complete abandonment of your responsibilities as a parent. You're not going to say to your 3-year-old, "Make your own way into town – there's a regular bus service. You'll thank me for this in years to come when you've scaled Everest."

But, there does come a point when parents need to see their children through different eyes and allow them to grow in responsibility.

The truth is ...

Kindness can sometimes kill confidence.

You can only allow people to grow when you withdraw some of your support and help them to discover their own internal resources to cope and survive. That doesn't mean that you abandon them – you don't withdraw *all* your support. But ultimately, if they are to learn how to fly they must first leave the nest.

What to Do if Your Mum was an Awfuliser

∞ Whether the Awfuliser was your mum, your dad, your granny, your uncle or your aunt, remember that their behaviour is not the sole reason for the person you are today.

∞ How you were brought up might not always have helped you develop your self-confidence, but people's behaviour towards you isn't definitive. Your destiny isn't determined by the actions of others but by how you respond to those actions.

∞ Remember, people often act out of ignorance rather than deliberate intention. They often repeat the same mistakes their parents made. Just make sure that you don't.

∞ Remind yourself that your parents (or care givers) are flawed – just like you.

∞ To create a sense of balance and perspective, think of three things a parent did for you that you really value and appreciate.

What to Do if *You're* an Awfuliser

We've spent some time examining the impact an Awfuliser can have on us. But I'm also conscious that we ourselves might also have a tendency to Awfulise. And if we do, we in turn can be affecting the confidence of those around us.

So if you recognize that you're an Awfuliser, what can you do? First, remember that the truth is ...

> You can't manage the past. You can only focus on today and determine that tomorrow will be better.

The key is to become more aware of when you're awfulising. You may still have a tendency to look on the downside of a situation, but that doesn't mean you have to automatically share those thoughts with other people. You may think it – but you don't have to express it.

(I explore the concept of Awfulisers in more detail in a previous book, *SUMO (Shut Up, Move On) Your Relationships, How to Handle Not Strangle the People You Live and Work With*.)

Criticism, Acceptance and Self-Confidence

Too much kindness as we have seen can actually stifle our development when well-meaning people help us avoid uncomfortable situations. This in turn means rather than learning how to face a challenge, and in doing so develop our confidence, we are instead rescued from the very situations that could benefit us in the long term.

However, on the flip side, too much criticism can wreak havoc with our self-esteem and personal confidence. Some people have a bizarre belief that the best way to build someone up is to constantly put them down. They buy into the philosophy that whatever doesn't kill you makes you stronger.

I disagree.

Big time.

Constant criticism, particularly when you're younger, can undermine your sense of self-worth and sow the seeds of behaviour that is constantly seeking acceptance and approval.

Sometimes that yearning for approval can lead to inappropriate and risky behaviour, particularly in our teenage years.

Others can be driven by an almost inner obsession to demonstrate their value. They have wrongly learnt that achievement is the *only* real grounds for acceptance. Therefore setbacks and failures are interpreted as a full frontal attack on their self-worth.

Now it's undeniable that our identity is wrapped up in some way with our accomplishments but some people believe they are *only* of worth if...

I am successful in what I do.

I never make mistakes.

People constantly praise me for my achievements.

I am clearly better than others.

Such a set of beliefs, even if we're not conscious of them, can see our confidence dive when we fail to live up to them.

Now I want my children to achieve in life. Make no mistake about that. And clearly achieving success in life does boost our self-confidence.

But *some* parents, perhaps driven by their own insecurities and sense of inadequacy, embark upon a crusade of wanting their children to constantly succeed. In doing so they send, unintentionally I appreciate, mixed messages to their children, who become conditioned to believe the following life equation:

Success+approval=acceptance and self-worth

Which may, at a superficial level, seem absolutely fine.

When we're being successful.

But what happens when we're not?

What happens when we don't live up to our parents or other people's expectations?

What happens when we disappoint or fail?

Are we then a failure?

A disappointment?

Is my self-worth linked solely to my ability to succeed?

So what happens when I don't achieve?

When I don't succeed?

Will you accept me anyway?

For who I am.

Not solely for what I do?

Am I to be celebrated for my being or for my performing?

Am I a human being

or

a human performing?

Am I like the seal at the water show, sustained by the applause of the crowd and the short-term rewards of my trainer?

Or am I more than that?

Of course I want my children to do well. Of course I want them to seize life's opportunities and to fulfil their potential.

Life is a privilege. It's not to be wasted.

But I also want my children to know that as their father I love them.

Full stop.

No 'if's.

No 'but's.

No 'as long as you meet a certain standard'.

Or live up to my expectations.

You're simply loved

For who

you

are.

End of story.

The truth is...

Children thrive on challenges. They're sustained by encouragement. They're crushed through continual criticism.

The Personal Stuff

I'm far from a perfect parent. Everyone who knows me would vouch for that. My own two children certainly would.

But I'm still working at it. I accept my failings but I also want to learn from them. You see being a parent doesn't stop until the day you die. It's not simply about how you were when your children were young.

You can repair the damage. You can right some wrongs.

I find that encouraging.

There's hope for me yet.

Because when my children were toddlers I feel that was not my finest hour. There were days when I struggled to cope.

Helen, however, was brilliant.

She made up for my shortcomings.

She was there when I wasn't.

She encouraged when I criticized.

She was patient.

I was a stress head.

She had her moments. None of us are perfect.

And maybe that's the important thing here.

None of us are

perfect.

No one.

Ever.

We've all made mistakes.

Said things we regret.

Lost it a little.

Lost it a lot.

But if you're like me your behaviour has often been borne out of good intentions and the recognition that raising children is hard.

Very hard at times.

So as time has gone on, as my children have got older, I've reflected more on my behaviours. I now realize the outcomes I experience are influenced considerably by my responses.

I've become more encouraging.

I'm less critical.

I still like to challenge.

My kids still have boundaries.

So how have I communicated that my love and approval of my kids is not solely dependent on their achievements?

Well one area Helen and I decided to address was to reward our children for their efforts rather than their results.

Exams are a case in point.

My son and daughter have had quite a few recently.

We want them to do well.

We support them all we can.

And when they've worked hard (which they have, up until this point anyway) we reward them.

Before their results are out.

Not after.

We celebrated when my son did well in his exams but by then he had already received his reward. We wanted to recognize the work he had put into the exams before he took them. I guess you could say we were recognising his character rather than his performance. In fact, we still look fondly back at the photo of him as a 16-year-old tucking into his McDonald's Happy Meal.

Just kidding.

We lost the photo.

The truth is...

> Value people, particularly children, for who they are, not simply for what they achieve.

Clearly this section is about how our upbringing has influenced our confidence and sense of worth. In the workplace the harsh realities of life are that we do need to perform and effort alone is not the criteria on which success is measured. Results are.

However, the most effective way to prepare ourselves and our children for the challenges of living and working in the 21st century is to operate from a sense of stability and security. To operate from a place of insecurity and poor self-worth gets you a lifelong pass on the extreme roller-coaster ride of life. It might seem exciting

but it's not.

Believe me.

In fact it's quite exhausting.

It's unfulfilling.

And ultimately

unsustainable.

So make sure you read on and find ways to trade in your pass for a far more enjoyable and still exciting ride, by learning to value yourself not just for what you achieve but for being who you are.

That's one aspect of your past that may have led to your self-confidence being eroded or not allowed to flourish. But that's enough navel-gazing in terms of your upbringing. It's time to explore how other people outside of your family may also have contributed to your lack of confidence.

in A Nutshell

∞ Your past experiences can make you bitter or better.

∞ Playing the "Explain Game" is helpful. Playing the "Blame Game" isn't.

∞ Beliefs can have a profound affect on you, and they don't have to be true to be powerful.

∞ How you're brought up can influence your beliefs and your self-confidence.

∞ Good intentions mixed with ignorance can lead to negative outcomes.

∞ Parents and other family members can pass on negative hand-me-down attitudes.

∞ Praise and acceptance solely for our achievements can actually undermine our self-worth.

4 Who Crushed Your Confidence? Other Influences

You're about to discover

How your
school days
affect your con-
fidence.

How the media distorts
reality and influences your
confidence.

Why you can undermine your own
self-confidence.

How Your School Days Affect Your Confidence

So far we've explored the power of beliefs and how they can affect your confidence. Our focus has been on the negative impact of beliefs, but they can also be very positive and life-affirming.

I came across an article in *Reader's Digest* about the actor Denzel Washington. He talked about how the key to much of his success was self-confidence and how he'd been helped by teachers as he grew up.

He recalled his youth group leader, Charlie White, saying to him one day, "Denzel, with your intelligence, you can do anything you want."

Washington added, "I was ten years old at the time, but I never forgot what he said. You never know the power of words when you speak to young people."

Clearly, those formative years as we're growing up can have a huge impact on us.

Most of us spend at least ten years at school. Isn't it interesting how many of those experiences you had then you can still vividly remember now? Certain teachers stand out, some for positive reasons but others for exactly the opposite. Who you spent time with in the playground or after school will also have influenced your outlook on life and on yourself.

Pit Stop

∞ Think of three positive memories from school. How did these experiences affect you?

∞ Which negative experiences spring to mind? How did those experiences affect you?

Perhaps the best way to explore the impact of people during your school days is to focus on some personal stories.

The Personal Stuff

School for me was a mixed bag. My confidence was boosted when I won several speaking competitions and took part in a number of school drama productions. And I have some positive memories of a number of teachers, particularly Mr Dart. He was my Maths teacher and his support and encouragement in a subject I struggled to master are something I remain hugely grateful for. Even now as I think about him, I smile.

Hopefully you had teachers like Mr Dart. It's important that you remind yourself of people like that in order to maintain your perspective.

However, this is a chapter about someone crushing your confidence and one teacher sadly, though I'm sure unintentionally, did precisely that to me.

In 1980 I was 15 years old and sitting my high school examinations. Up to that point, no one in our family had ever passed an "O" level (as GCSEs were known then). This situation certainly wasn't helped by the fact that no one in our family had ever actually sat an "O" level exam.

Initially I passed four "O" levels. It would have been five, but my pot blew up in the school kiln, so I missed out on Pottery (I got an unclassified, which is quite an achievement in that subject!). I was gutted. Therapy helped.

I scraped into the Sixth form to do my "A" levels. I realized that I'd done quite well to get that far in my academic journey. My mum was proud of me anyway. She thought I was a child genius. But there was also a sense that I had reached my academic ceiling. If you come from a background where even a single "O" level was an achievement, then I guess talk of doing a degree was strictly off limits.

So there I was studying for my "A" levels. But while most if not all my classmates were deciding which university or polytechnic to apply for (then they were different institutions), I was lining up job interviews to work in a bank. Occasionally, during lessons my mates would be filling in application forms for various academic institutions. Initially I was quite relieved at not having to go through such a chore. However, the more they talked about what degree they hoped to take and whereabouts in the country they hoped to study, the less appealing working as a bank clerk in Chorlton-cum-Hardy seemed.

At the time polytechnics had a more vocational edge to their degrees and some people, although not everyone, chose to apply to one if they weren't confident that they would get sufficiently high grades to go to university. One day I had an epiphany (which, in case you're wondering, isn't some medical condition). What was to stop me exploring the possibility of going to a polytechnic, even if I did have a job lined up in a bank?

I got quite excited at the idea. Suddenly the thought of continuing my studies, if I could find the right course, grew rather appealing. I decided to check it out with a teacher.

It's been nearly 30 years since the following conversation took place, but I remember it like it was yesterday. Here's how it went.

"Sir, have you got a minute?"

Mr Wakefield (to save his embarrassment, that's not his real name) looked briefly at his watch and then at me. "Yes, what is it McGee?" (None of the male teachers called us by our first names.)

"Sir, I was just wondering," I said in a slightly hesitant manner. "I realize I'm not good enough to go to university …"

"Yes," interrupted Mr Wakefield in a "that's-kind-of-obvious-don't-you-think" tone of voice.

"But do you think I should apply to go to polytechnic?"

"Haven't you got a job lined up in the bank?"

"Oh yes, sir. I start in July, once I've finished my 'A' levels. I just thought it might be good to have a plan B."

Mr Wakefield was clearly in a hurry and I sensed he hadn't expected to be having such a conversation with me. He seemed distracted and slightly caught off guard.

"Well McGee, if I was you I'd stick with the bank. Now, was there anything else?" As if sensing my disappointment from my lack of response, he added, "To be honest,

McGee, who knows what the job market will be like in the next three years. The bank's your best option."

I shrugged and said, "Fine, I realize it was a crazy idea, I just thought …"

Our conversation was over in less than 30 seconds. It influenced the next 12 months of my life.

As I walked away from Mr Wakefield, the small flame of my academic aspirations flickered out. I didn't question his opinion, because I trusted him. What had I been thinking? I'd just been deluding myself. Time to prepare for my life in the bank and leave polytechnics and universities to the really bright kids in my class.

I hated the bank. Within two weeks of joining I was going for job interviews in my lunch hour.

Four weeks later I got my "A" level results. They were better than expected. They were good enough to get into polytechnic. In fact, they were good enough to go to university.

The power of words, hey? The Book of Proverbs says they have the power to bring life or death. Mr Wakefield's words weren't fatal, but they did have a significant impact.

Pit Stop

- ∞ Think about a teacher who inspired or encouraged you. What was their name?
- ∞ How did they help you?
- ∞ Think about a teacher who had a negative impact on you. What was it that they said or did that caused this impact?
- ∞ How did that affect you at the time? What have been the long-term ramifications?

Many of the personal issues you face today stem from your experiences in the past, whether they were due to an over-protective parent or a thoughtless teacher. Sometimes an event can lead to some major long-term damage, but thankfully the effect's often minor, as the next story illustrates.

The Personal Stuff

Helen rarely makes pastry these days. That stems from a cookery class at school. Helen and her classmates were making pastry. Her friend Debbie asked the teacher for feedback as she rubbed the butter into the flour. The teacher was impressed.

Helen sought similar reassurance. Looking at her efforts, the teacher gathered the rest of the class around the two girls. Turning to Debbie's pastry she said, "Here's how it should look girls." Then of Helen's pastry she added, "and here's how it *shouldn't* look."

It was a humiliating experience for a relatively shy teenage girl. Even though Helen is a fairly confident person in other areas, it took her a long time to gain any self-confidence in pastry making.

Teachers do an incredibly challenging and difficult job and they get blamed for a lot. My goal isn't to add to that blame, but simply to raise awareness that how they behave can have a profound long-term effect on young people, both positively and negatively – even if it's only in relation to pastry making.

However, it's not just teachers or parents who influence your beliefs and affect your confidence. Let's look at another key influence.

How the Media can Influence Your Self-Confidence

Hitler knew it, so did Churchill, so did Sir Bob Geldof.

Companies now spend millions of pounds on it.

Quite simply, if you want to change, shape and influence people's minds, then the media can be your most powerful weapon.

You see, the media doesn't merely transmit information. The media shapes our culture. It reinforces stereotypes. It subtly influences our views of what is acceptable and good and what is unacceptable and bad.

The media is powerful. It can arouse and awaken the conscience of a nation. It can also distort the truth and deceive people in doing so.

The media can also influence the beliefs you hold about yourself. And not all those beliefs are as empowering as they might first appear.

"I must be slim."
"I must be popular."
"I must have the latest fashion accessory."
"I must be cool, and be seen to be cool."

I guess all the above seem fine when you're slim, popular, wear the latest fashions and people think you're cool. But what if you're not?

What if your weight is an issue? What if your body shape is not OK in your culture, even though it may be in others?

What if you're not so popular?

What if you can't afford to keep up with the latest fashions?

What if you're obsessed with what other people think about you?

You see, on a deserted desert island you might feel OK about yourself. But you're not on that island.

So now there's a nagging sense of insecurity based on comparing yourself with other people. Now there's a sense of feeling inadequate because of what some parts of the media purport is OK and acceptable in terms of how you should look and behave.

Subtly and gradually

the media can chip away at your confidence.

There's another way in which the media influences you – bad news can arouse, titillate and undermine your confidence.

The death of Diana, Princess of Wales in 1997 was tragic news – but in the short term it proved to be good news for the media. There were record sales of newspapers in the UK in the aftermath of her death. Quite simply, bad news sells. That's true the whole world over.

And let's be honest, what arouses your interest more? Hearing about a friend who's been happily married for the last 20 years, or discovering that they've been having an affair and their partner has just found out? The former might please you, but the latter arouses your intrigue and curiosity far, far more.

Therefore the media can argue, perhaps quite rightly, that they only publish or televise what people want to read or hear about. Ultimately they're competing for our attention and to do so they have to shout loudly. Sometimes that means sensationalizing and exaggerating the real facts in order to be heard.

However, the purpose of this discussion is not to examine the ethics of the media. What is under scrutiny is how the media can, in some cases, erode your self-confidence by distorting your view of reality. Let me explain.

Imagine that you find yourself out of work. So much of your self-worth and esteem can be wrapped up in your job, and now you don't have one. How are you feeling?

With that in mind, you might find the next story particularly interesting.

The Personal Stuff

In the early 1990s I worked with an organization that was set up to help coal miners who'd lost their jobs due to the closures of their collieries. My role was to offer advice and support in writing CVs, completing application forms and preparing for job interviews. I was also there to provide some psychological support and encouragement.

For the majority of the men, working in the mining industry was the only job they'd had since leaving school. Some were quite positive about their future and saw this as a new beginning. But for some their confidence was shattered. Their expectations of finding work were minimal. Their sense of pride and self-respect had been left behind in the now redundant coal mines.

My goal was to offer some hope and to help them gradually rebuild their fragile confidence and self-esteem.

"But there's no bloody jobs." That was a phrase I heard over and over and over again.

The economy at the time was certainly not booming, but the pessimistic outlook of some of the miners was fed and reinforced by the media. Bad news doesn't only sell, it can also influence a person's outlook and self-belief.

My aim was to show them that the picture of the world their local press painted was not in fact the whole story. I didn't have to look far to prove my point.

A supermarket chain was looking to build a distribution centre, and in doing so would create 800 new jobs. The company was looking at two sites. Site A was close to a former colliery in the North West of England and ex-miners would be given priority for jobs. Site B was also in the North West of England, less than 20 miles away from Site A. The supermarket eventually chose Site A as the most suitable location for its distribution centre. Good news for the people seeking work who lived in the area, but bad news for those people hoping to see the centre located at Site B.

So how did the local press cover the story? The paper that published in the area closest to Site A (where the distribution centre was to be built) led with a front-page story of how a Christmas tree had been set ablaze in a pub. The pub was evacuated. Nobody died. Nobody was injured. Also on the front page was a small piece about how a 71-year-old pensioner had ended up in hospital after she dropped a frozen turkey on her foot. (Clearly the readers of this paper love their diet of cutting-edge news.) Fortunately her foot wasn't broken. (That must have been a relief to the readers.)

And the piece about the creation of 800 new jobs? That was on page three. Even then it wasn't the main story on the page. Although politicians can be accused of wanting to bury bad news, it seems the media can be equally guilty of burying good news.

So what about the people buying the local paper that published close to Site B? (That's the site that hadn't been chosen for the distribution centre.) Where did they read about the same story? Page three?

Are you kidding? You've probably guessed.

The news that the supermarket distribution centre wasn't to be located in their area was front-page news. I've still got a copy of the respective papers. The headline read:

> ## 800 JOBS LOST

It went on to say that hopes of a jobs bonanza had been crushed (interesting word to use, don't you think?) with the decision that the distribution centre wasn't to be built in their area.

Bad news sells.

But it also distorts our picture of reality.

When you're looking for work and your confidence is low, it's perhaps understandable that your sense of hope and optimism is further diminished when you switch on the news, turn on the radio, log onto the internet or pick up the paper. I wonder, is it time to change your media diet?

 Pit Stop

- ∞ How much news do you consume in a day?
- ∞ On reflection, how does it affect your mood and morale?
- ∞ When was the last time you watched or read anything that inspired you? What was it?

How You can Undermine Your Own Confidence

So far we've seen how a combination of factors can erode and perhaps ultimately crush your confidence. Parents can, so too can teachers, and even the media can play its part.

Let me say again: my goal in exploring these factors has not been to play the blame game, but to gain some understanding of why you might lack confidence in certain areas of your life.

Now onto our final factor that can contribute to the undermining of your confidence – yourself.

A question I often ask my audiences is, "Who is the most important person you will ever talk to?"

The answer?

Yourself.

The conversations you have with yourself, your internal self-talk, can have a significant impact on how you feel and behave. Put quite simply, your internal self-talk can either reinforce your negative beliefs or help replace them with more positive, empowering ones.

In my book *S.U.M.O. (Shut Up, Move On)*, I explored the T.E.A.R. process. It's worth revisiting briefly here:

T – Thinking (your internal dialogue, your self-talk, your thoughts).
↓
E – Emotions (your feelings, which are influenced by what you're thinking about).
↓
A – Actions (your behaviour, the things you do or don't do).
↓
R – Results (the outcomes of your actions).

The T.E.A.R. process is based on cognitive behavioural therapy or CBT, and it aims to illustrate the importance and impact of your thinking. (Psychotherapist Aaron Beck helped develop CBT and believes that the way in which you think about a situation affects how you act. In turn, your actions can affect how you think and feel.)

When people talk about confidence, they typically associate it with "feelings" (or emotions). They often say either:

"I feel very confident."

or

"I don't feel very confident."

They rarely say:

"I'm thinking in a confident way."

or

"My thinking is leading me to feel less confident."

However, despite the language you may use, those feelings of confidence or lack of confidence are strongly associated with your thinking, or your internal self-talk.

In Chapter 6, "How to be your own best mate", we explore how to make your thinking work for you. However, at this point it's important for you to recognize that the conversations you have with yourself can potentially undermine your self-confidence.

What do you say when you talk to yourself?

Can you relate to any of the following phrases?

"I'm hopeless at ..."
"I'll never be any good at ..."
"I absolutely hate having to ..."
"I'm always forgetting to ..."

All these statements are ways in which you articulate the beliefs you have about yourself.

To be honest, it would be surprising if you haven't ever said any of the above. So if that's the case, am I suggesting that the whole world is going around undermining their own self-confidence?

No.

The issue is not whether you have ever said these phrases to yourself, but more importantly, *how often* you say them, and how much you *believe* them. You see, when you hear something often enough (even if it's said purely through habit), you start to believe it.

If you think negatively about yourself and your potential, it will gradually begin to affect how you're feeling and slowly erode or undermine your confidence.

Interestingly, although the above may seem fairly obvious, few of us are aware of how critical our thinking actually is. In fact, rarely do we take time out to think about how we think.

If I were to ask you which side of your mouth you tend to chew your food on, most people would have to take a moment to think about their answer.

Why? After all, you do it all the time.

The reason?

Because you do it without consciously thinking about it. You eat without thinking about how you're eating.

The same goes for your thinking. You're often not consciously aware of how your thinking is affecting your feelings – or the fact that you can change and take control of your thoughts.

The truth is ...

> If you can change your thinking, you can change how you're feeling.

Pit Stop

∞ What are some of the negative phrases you say to yourself?

∞ How often do you say them? Daily? Weekly? Or rarely?

∞ On a scale of 1–10, how much do you actually believe them?

The Personal Stuff

My wife Helen and I recently met Claire at a friend's party. I had known her at university but hadn't seen her in over 20 years.

Let me tell you a little about Claire. She's physically very attractive. She has a relatively outgoing personality and is easy to get on with. She's in good shape and enjoys running. When you're at a party full of strangers she would seem like the ideal person to hang out with (and that's not just my perspective – Helen would think the same).

Except for one thing.

Claire has a rather irritating habit.

She constantly puts herself down.

A certain degree of self-deprecation, particularly when dished out with a large dose of humour, can be quite endearing. But if Claire was an Italian meal then the only dish available would be spaghetti. It's certainly nice as part of a main course, but it loses all its appeal when nothing else accompanies it.

I soon felt bloated from her negativity. It was a habit I first noticed when Claire and I were students, but I thought after 20 years she'd have grown out of it. I was wrong.

"I'm a person with a great future behind me," she remarked. An amusing comment if taken as a one-off, but further comments followed. Her comments seemed born out of a belief about herself that could be summed up as follows: "I'm not an OK person."

Her burden of insecurity seemed heavy on her shoulders. She seemed unhappy.

She talked about her career as a teacher and how she felt she'd not reached her potential. I wanted to agree with her. I wanted to say that the reason she hadn't reached her potential was not down to a lack of ability or opportunity, but due to a lack of self-belief and confidence.

I've no idea why Claire felt this way about herself but I do know that whatever the cause, Claire had bought into a lie and was continuing to maintain it.

The truth is ...

Holding negative beliefs about yourself can put the brakes on you making a breakthrough.

Pit Stop

∞ Who do you know who reminds you of Claire?
∞ Can you relate to her at all?
∞ What's the one negative belief about yourself that you've bought into and are helping to maintain?

in A Nutshell

∞ People develop confidence over time. This comes through life experiences and through the support, advice and encouragement of others.

∞ Our experiences at school, particularly our interactions with teachers and classmates, can have a profound long-term effect on us.

∞ The media can quite subtly affect how we see ourselves. It can influence our view of what is "normal" and distort our view of reality.

∞ We can be our own worst enemy by reinforcing negative self-beliefs by the thoughts we have about ourselves.

Understanding the reasons for our lack of confidence places us in a better position to do something about it. It's not fate that's given us low self-confidence, there are causes. And revealing what those causes were places us in a position to move forward and discover some solutions.

Now it's time for a change of focus. The rest of this book is dedicated to showing you how to rebuild and strengthen your confidence in order to fulfill your potential and to make the most of life. And if your confidence takes a knock, you'll discover how to prevent that becoming a permanent blow.

So let's move on from why confidence is such a big deal and who might have crushed it, to learning how a small change – maybe as little as 10 percent – can make a big difference.

SECTION TWO

The Stuff that Will Really Help

5 You'll Get By with a Little Help from Your Friends

You're about to discover

Why your
ability to
succeed is
inextricably linked
to the support you get
from others.

The four roles people play to
help you grow in confidence and
achieve your potential.

The pitfalls and dangers when you have
unbalanced support from people.

How to get help from people you don't
know and will never meet.

The Beatles had a hit song in 1967 called "With a Little Help from My Friends." They probably didn't realize it at the time, but they were promoting a truth that can have a major impact on our levels of health, happiness and self-confidence.

The truth is ...

Confidence may be an inside job, but it requires outside help.

Battling through life believing that you and you alone are wholly responsible for your success is, to put it bluntly, a lie.

Perhaps you're thinking that asking for help from others is a sign of weakness.

It isn't.

It's a reality.

And yes, there's much you can do to help yourself increase your self-confidence, but ultimately the journey is easier and probably quicker when you enlist the help of others.

Desperately Dependent?

As humans, we are one of the most needy and vulnerable of the animal species when we're born. We are totally dependent on the care, protection and provision of others. No support equals no survival. I'm not suggesting that other animals don't require caring for when they're born, but the level of care required and the length of time it's required for is usually far less than for the human species.

However, as we develop we increasingly like our independence and freedom. And that's not without its challenges. The cause of much of the conflict in families comes when a teenager seeks to assert their independence and break free from their parents' influence, while still being dependent on them (at least in most cases) for food, shelter and quite often money!

So yes, we need freedom to grow – but freedom does not equate to going it alone. Just as learning to ride a bike usually requires stabilizers until we gain our balance, so people need stabilizers or supporters to help them master life's challenges.

The truth is ...

None of us have got it together. But together we've got it.

Where does Your Support Come from?

The rower Steven Redgrave won five gold medals over five consecutive Olympic Games. It's a remarkable achievement. I guess when it came to rowing during that period, Steve was very confident of achieving success.

He's crossed the line first on five separate occasions, but here's my question.

How many times was he alone in the boat when he crossed the line?

The answer?

Never.

On every single occasion Redgrave was in the boat with at least one other person. His success, however remarkable, was not achieved solely through his own strength, skill and expertise, but with the support of others. And there were plenty of other people who never stepped inside that boat who also contributed significantly to his success.

Redgrave was confident of success not just because of his own ability but also because of the support of others. Put quite simply: without them, there would be no gold medals.

So who helps you achieve success? Who helps you increase your levels of self-confidence?

Interestingly, the type of people who may be responsible for crushing or eroding your confidence could equally be the people who help nurture and grow it:

Parents
Other family members
Teachers
Friends at school
Bosses

In reflecting on the kind of help we need from people in order to boost our confidence and our ability to succeed in life, I identified four roles people play (it's possible, although unlikely, that one person may play all four). Here are the names I've given to each one: Cheerleader, Challenger, Coach and Confidant. Let's explore how each of these provides unique support.

The Cheerleader

These are the people who seek to encourage you. They're the people who when they introduce you to others at a social gathering don't just use your name, but are likely to "big you up" as they do so. They believe in you and your abilities to succeed. When you're feeling down, a Cheerleader's intention is not so much to empathize with your situation but to help pick you up. They offer hope.

Going back to the T.E.A.R. (Thinking, Emotions, Actions, Results) process, they can help influence your Thinking about yourself and your situation in such a way that Emotionally you feel more positive and confident. A Cheerleader might not be able to advise you on the Actions you need to take to get the Results you want, but they can help you to believe enough in yourself to explore what actions are required.

The upside of a Cheerleader

∞ They're great encouragers.
∞ They can generate optimism within you about the future.
∞ They can be a great antidote when you're feeling low.
∞ They remind you of your successes.

The downside of a Cheerleader

∞ They may encourage an unrealistically high view of yourself and your capabilities. This could lead to self-delusion and not self-development.
∞ They may lack the necessary insight and experience to provide real support in a situation.
∞ They're unlikely to allow you sufficient downtime when you've experienced a setback and could feel uncomfortable around you when you're angry or upset.
∞ They can generate the necessary enthusiasm for a task, but lack the knowledge to help you accomplish it.

Cheerleaders can help you believe it's possible to climb the mountain, but they can't provide you with the equipment to get to the summit.

In conversation with a Cheerleader

You: "Well, I've had some bad news. Looks like they'll be laying off people at work. It's going to be a struggle finding anything at the moment."

Cheerleader: "But Paul, you've got an amazingly wide range of skills. Most employers would be thrilled to have you working for them."

You: "I'm not so sure. I've been with this company for ten years. I'm dreading having to go for interviews."

Cheerleader: "Look Paul, I think you're underestimating your worth. You've achieved loads in this job – another employer is bound to spot that."

You: "But what about the interviews?"

Cheerleader: "Relax. You're getting this out of perspective. They're not as bad as you think. I've got total confidence in you mate. You'll be fine."

Pit Stop

∞ Who are the Cheerleaders in your life?
∞ How do they help you?
∞ Are you a cheerleader to anyone?
∞ How can you consciously be more of a Cheerleader to other people?

The Challenger

These are the people who question your motives, plans and dreams. Their goal is not to discourage you, but to help you explore in more depth what you're actually trying to achieve and what the benefit will be when you do so. They raise questions you've never considered. They can take your thinking to a new level.

The upside of a Challenger

∞ They help you realize that success is not just because of positive energy but that there's also a need for a thought-through strategy.
∞ They can help direct and focus your enthusiasm as well as question its validity and sustainability.
∞ They can both widen your thinking to explore new possibilities and narrow your thinking to achieve your goal.
∞ If your progress is slow they're unlikely simply to encourage you to press on, but to ask for reasons for the delay in your progress.

The downside of a Challenger

∞ Their seeming lack of positive enthusiasm towards you may at times appear as if their motives are questionable. The question may arise, "Are they trying to help me or to bring me down?"
∞ They may challenge you when emotionally you're not in a good place to be challenged, particularly after a setback.
∞ They may not provide the necessary encouragement when required.

∞ Occasionally their questioning, especially around considering other possibilities, may actually bring confusion and not clarity.

Challengers can help you understand more fully how big the mountain is and that there are several ways to reach the top, but crucially they might not be able to show you *how* to climb it.

In conversation with a Challenger

You: "Well, I've completed my sales proposal. I'm fairly confident we'll get the business."

Challenger: "How have you gone about it?"

You: "I've just used the usual format. It's always worked before."

Challenger: "Fine. But why are you so confident it will work on this occasion? Have you gone through it with anyone?"

You: "Well, not yet, no. But I've done dozens of proposals in the past."

Challenger: "I'm not suggesting you haven't. This might be exactly what your client was looking for, but just to be on the safe side would it help if I had a look over it?"

You: "Yeah that would be great. Thanks."

Challenger: "Let's start with the attitude that however good it is, there's probably going to be a way to improve it. Agreed?"

You: "I guess so."

Pit Stop

∞ Who are the Challengers in your life? (If you can't think of any, would it be useful to give certain people permission to challenge you when appropriate?)
∞ Identify one person who you could be more of a support to by being their Challenger.

The Coach

These people could be a combination of Cheerleader and Challenger. Their focus above all tends to be on the "A" in the T.E.A.R. process: the Actions.

The Coach won't just challenge your thinking but help you to explore what tools you need in order to accomplish your goal. They will help you to look to your own internal resources and also examine the external opportunities available to you. The Coach will help you be clear and specific in the actions to take and hold you accountable as to when they're carried out. They may well be a resource expert for you themselves, or they will point you in the direction of where you will find them.

The upside of a Coach

∞ You will probably have a more formal relationship with a Coach (many people pay for their services), which puts things on a more professional footing. Therefore there's an expectation that they will provide more structure and focus to your conversations as well as an increased expectation regarding their input.

∞ They are more likely to challenge you than a well-meaning friend would do.

∞ As a follow-up or review is usually built into the relationship, they're also more able to hold you accountable regarding your progress (or lack of it).

∞ Confidence can come from them being a sounding board and because you have explored your issues with them.

∞ Their detached perspective can provide a clarity that is not clouded by emotional involvement.

The downside of a Coach

∞ The role requires a range of skills that you're unlikely to find in a well-meaning friend. Therefore the relationship is more likely, although not necessarily, based on a professional fee paying basis (unless your organization provides you with a Coach). Cost may also play a part in how long the Coaching lasts.

∞ Because they're unlikely to be a friend the Coach can offer a detached perspective on your situation, although this detachment could also be viewed as uncaring.

∞ Your interaction is likely to be built on an agreement between two parties and not out of a friendship and that itself can obviously influence the dynamics of your relationship.

A Coach will help you find a way up the mountain. They may even accompany you on the journey. The Coach will show you the tools to use and how to use them, but they might not necessarily provide you with the motivation or the inspiration to make the climb.

In conversation with a Coach

You: "I'm really struggling with keeping to my New Year resolutions. By the end of the first week of January I'm already beginning to feel a failure."

Coach: "Why do you think that is?"

You: "Well, I start off all enthusiastic but then I get a setback or something happens at work and before I know it I'm back to square one."

Coach: "And because of that you feel a failure?"

You: "Yeah."

Coach: "OK, let's see what we can do to improve this situation and achieve some success. That is something you want to do, isn't it?"

You: "Absolutely."

Coach: "Good. Well, out of all your New Year resolutions, which one is perhaps the most important to you right now?"

You: "Losing weight, definitely."

Coach: "So how about we look at that one for the moment and put all the others to one side?"

You: "Sounds good to me."

Coach: "OK. Let's start by finding out your current weight and then look at what your overall goal is. Then we can look at ways to help you achieve this goal."

∞ Do you have a Coach? (Don't get too hung up by the title. My daughter gets dance and singing lessons. The people who support her are called teachers and she gets support on both a group and a one-to-one basis.)

∞ If you had to identify one specific area of your life where a Coach could help you, what would it be?

∞ What would be the benefits to you if you could develop and improve in that specific area?

The Confidant

These are the people you trust. Their support comes not because of their ability but because of their integrity. A Confidant listens. They are not there to advise you, but to provide you with emotional support. Their encouragement comes from their willingness to offer empathy and understanding. They may challenge you occasionally and may at times be your Cheerleader, but that is not their primary role.

The upside of a Confidant

∞ They are the people to whom you can offload. They're easy to have as friends and supporters because you can simply talk to them. You don't have to answer their questions about your plans and motives. That is not their role.

∞ When you're feeling down they can provide perspective, not through their answers but because they give
you an opportunity to express and articulate your frus-
trations and concerns. And as you do so, invariably
you're able to become calmer and clearer about your
situation.

∞ A Confidant above all gives you time and space, and this
in itself can provide perspective and renew your confidence and sense of optimism.

The downside of a Confidant

∞ When you're looking for advice or a strategy for how to
deal with an issue, the Confidant is not the person
for you. Their support is invaluable, but they cannot
necessarily provide the direction to help you move
forward.

∞ It is possible that having confided in them you may still
feel frustration at your lack of progress or ability to
know what your next step will be.

You can share your dream about climbing the mountain,
you can even talk at great length about your failed attempts
to climb it so far, but a Confidant's role is not to provide
you with the motivation, tools or strategy to help you fulfill
your dream.

In conversation with a Confidant

You: "I've had a nightmare at work today."

Confidant: "In what way?"

You: "Oh it's Kathy, my boss. She's always picking on me."

Confidant: "How do you mean?"

You: "Well, you name it she does it."

Confidant: "Does she pick on anyone else?"

You: "Actually she tends to pick on everyone at the moment."

Confidant: "If she's anything like me, it sounds like she's either hormonal or under a lot of pressure!"

You: "It's probably both. To be fair, she is under a lot of pressure at the moment – there are quite a few people off work. To be honest, she's not like that with me all the time. She can be quite human sometimes!"

Confidant: "But if you did have an issue with her, could you talk to her?"

You: "Oh yeah. Absolutely. Actually I don't know what I'm moaning about really. I'm more than capable of dealing with it when I think about it."

Confidant: "Well, you know I'm always here if you want to talk anything through."

∞ Who's your Confidant? In what specific ways do they help you?
∞ Who are you a Confidant to?
∞ Consider the skills required to be a Confidant. What would be your challenge in seeking to be one for someone else?

A Summary of the Roles

We all need help from others if we're going to grow in confidence. A word of advice, some encouragement, a listening ear or the challenge to aim higher could all make a big difference to our confidence in different situations. Here is a summary of the four roles and the upside and potential downside of their involvement in supporting us.

Cheerleader	Challenger
Upside	**Upside**
Great encourager	Questions your motives from a positive perspective
"Bigs you up"	
Believes in you	Helps you explore things in more depth
Picks you up from a setback	
Optimistic about your future	Raises questions you might not have considered
Reminds you of your successes	
	Helps take your thinking to a new level
	Helps you discover a strategy

Cheerleader	Challenger
Downside	**Downside**
May encourage an unrealistically high view of yourself	Their motives may be questioned at times
May lack the insight or skills to help you	May challenge you at a time when emotionally you're not ready to be
May trivialize your setbacks	May not always provide the necessary encouragement
	Their questioning could bring confusion, not clarity, at times.

Coach	Confidant
Upside	**Upside**
Helps you explore the tools you require to achieve your goal	You trust these people
Helps you identify internal and external resources to help you achieve your goal	A great listener to whom you can offload
Could be a resource for you	Helps provide perspective through their calm approach
Can prove to be an excellent sounding board and able to provide an objective perspective	Gives you time and space to talk through your issues
	Doesn't provide answers but can help you to discover your own
Downside	**Downside**
You're unlikely to find all these skills in a friend	Usually unable to provide advice or a strategy
You may need to pay for their expertise	You may be frustrated with their inability to provide you with any answers
Their detached perspective could be viewed as uncaring	Sometimes it's not empathy that you need but a kick up the backside to go out and do something
The potential cost of their support may prove prohibitive	

The Beatles were Right

In the chorus of their hit song "Help!", The Beatles sing about how they need somebody – but not just anybody.

In order to develop your self-confidence you may need someone's help, but be careful who that person is. For instance:

∞ When you need a reality check, a Cheerleader won't be the most helpful person.
∞ When you're particularly lacking in confidence, a Challenger may make the situation worse.
∞ When you need a strategy, don't look to a Confidant.
∞ Rarely will you find a person within your circle of friends who has the skills of a Coach.

Different Roles for Different Folks

It's important to understand that people can play different roles

to different people

in different situations.

For example, to some people you may be a Cheerleader, but to others you may be a Challenger. Within my role as a Coach I can find myself also playing the role of Cheerleader or Challenger, depending on the person I'm coaching and their current level of confidence and competence (I'm much more likely to be a Cheerleader to someone lacking in confidence and ability than to someone who is already very confident and competent: one needs encouragement, the other needs the challenge to become even better).

The key is to realize that you can play different roles for people and likewise they can do the same for you.

The danger comes when we lack other people's support or when we have the input of only one of those roles.

For instance, a child whose parents constantly play the role of Challenger will over time see their confidence eroded. While their performance in a particular task may increase, their levels of self-confidence and self-acceptance may decrease. In this situation the child's confidence may be inextricably linked to their performance or competence and not to their intrinsic worth as a human being.

That's bad news.

Agree?

Likewise, arrogance and complacency can flourish when a person surrounds themselves with Cheerleaders and fails to have anyone in their world who acts as a Challenger.

Again, that's bad news for all concerned.

Self-Confidence

The Personal Stuff

Part of my self-confidence stems from the support and encouragement of my mum. Although she's played many roles in my life and would admit she hasn't always got it right, she has undoubtedly been my Cheerleader. She gets excited at any success I achieve, no matter how small, and has no hesitation in letting her friends know about my achievements. She can also be a Confidant, but unless she's teaching me how to make her legendary mince pies, she's definitely not my Coach.

But I also need my Challengers – in fact, I actively seek them out for certain projects. While writing *S.U.M.O. (Shut Up, Move On)*, I would send each completed chapter to four people for their input, ideas and feedback. They had permission to challenge and pull apart my work. In order to have the confidence that I'd written a good book, I needed them to challenge both my content and style. Four people telling me how wonderful my writing was would not have been particularly helpful. Having said that, occasional praise was always appreciated – they weren't banned from ever being my Cheerleader – it just wasn't their primary role.

I didn't always agree with all their feedback, but allowing myself and my work to be challenged helped increase my confidence and belief in what I'd written. I've gone through exactly the same process with this book and it's helped immensely (however, you will be the judge of whether my confidence in what I've written is misplaced or not).

Some would argue that you have to be relatively self-confident to allow someone to be your challenger and that a sign that people lack self-confidence is when they're unwilling to be challenged. Do you know anyone like that?

My friend Paul is unique because he has the ability to play all four roles in terms of how he relates to me. He's a Cheerleader for who I am as a person, but he's very much a Challenger of my work. Our relationship, though, has been forged over 20 years and in some respects he's earned the right to be my Challenger. I know his heart. I know his intentions.

I believe that the quality of my work is better and has more depth because of Paul's insights, comments and questions – and I'm more confident in what I do as a result.

Mind you, there are some people who want to play the Challenger in my life but without my permission! Maybe you've had a similar experience.

Having conducted a seminar in London, one woman wrote on the evaluation form "10 things I hated about today's trainer." My confidence felt crushed and I turned to Paul for his support. Sensing my anguish as I read out what she wrote, he replied, "I'm surprised she only spotted ten!"

Having used humour to defuse the situation, he then played the role of Confidant and allowed me to talk. His final comment still sticks with me, "Sometimes what people say is not so much about you, it's more a reflection of what's going on in their world at the time."

Paul does have his limitations in terms of what he can do to help me. Likewise, you'll need more than one person to help you grow and develop in your competence and confidence.

In the last few months there's another person who has become a huge support to Helen and me: Humphrey, our business Coach.

I started off my business as a one-man band. Then Helen joined me. But things have changed. The business has grown. We've taken on staff and associates and the launch of SUMO4Schools has been both exciting and challenging.

Helen and I have many skills, but we both lack some of the necessary skills and expertise to drive the business forward. Left to our own devices I'm fairly confident that our business would have continued to plod along steadily, but not achieve anything like its potential. That's how it can be for anyone when we lack the support we need in particular areas.

Can you relate to that at all?

We needed help. We needed somebody to hold our hand, give us a map and help us climb our mountain.

My friend Andy Bounds mentioned that the best financial business investment he had ever made came when he hired his business coach, Humphrey. We had our answer. Or to put it more bluntly, we had our Humphrey.

I'm now confident about the growth and success of our business because we have the support of someone with the competence and expertise that we lack.

Maybe that's what you need as well. Someone to take you to the next level. Someone who's strong where you're weak.

Just make sure that you have the right people to fulfil the four roles.

Pit Stop

∞ Out of the four roles of Cheerleader, Challenger, Coach and Confidant, which, if any, are you lacking input from?
∞ Are you surrounding yourself with people who all play a similar role? If so, what are the consequences?
∞ Could any of them play another role?
∞ How would that benefit you if they did?

Widening Your Circle of Friends

We've explored the roles people may play in our lives that ultimately can help us grow in confidence, but sometimes our "friend" might not come in the form of a person we actually know. I realize that might sound strange, so let me explain.

We can all learn lessons from people we've never met. Our inspiration can come from reading their book, or watching their DVD or listening to them on CD.

I read a lot. I listen to CDs when I'm driving. I gain ideas, insights and inspiration from people I've never met and in some cases am unlikely ever to meet (the fact that some of them are now dead settles the issue, I guess).

But I get by with a little help from my friends. And I'm not limiting those friends to being living, walking, talking human beings. To do so would be to limit the scope of input that people can have to my life.

∞ Who inspires you although you've never met them?
∞ Have you read, watched or listened to anything inspirational recently?
∞ If not, isn't it about time you did so?
∞ Go on then – do something about it.

The Personal Stuff

This is Sarah's story:

When I was made redundant, it's fair to say there were some dark moments and challenging times. I drew strength from family and friends, but I also drew confidence from a poem that I had on my wall.

The poem goes by two titles: "Thinking" and the more commonly used "The man who thinks he can." Here it is:

If you think you are beaten you are.
If you think you dare not, you don't.
If you'd like to win but think you can't,
It's almost certain you won't.

If you think you will lose, you've lost.
For out of the world you'll find,
Success begins with a fellow's will,
It's all in the state of the mind.

If you think you're outclassed you are.
You've got to think high to rise.

You've got to be sure of yourself
Before you can ever win a prize.

Life's battles don't always go
To the stronger or faster man.
But soon or late, the man who wins
Is the man who thinks he can.

Walter D. Wintle

The poem reminded me of the importance of self-belief and having a positive attitude to life. In a small yet significant way it helped boost my confidence – I hope it does the same for you too.

in A Nutshell

So you'll get by with a little help from your friends. In fact, you might not just get by – your friends can help you soar. Let's appreciate and value the roles others play in helping us and lets also be prepared to become that role for others who need to boost their own confidence.

The truth is that we all need Cheerleaders, Challengers, Coaches and Confidants at times. Remember, the key to success and increased confidence is not independence – doing it all on your own – but interdependence – doing it with the help of others. That small change in thinking could make a big difference to what you're able to achieve in life.

6 How to Be Your Own Best Mate

You're about to discover

Seven ideas on how
to avoid sabotaging
your confidence.

Why it's important to accept
that "flaws are us".

The need to go easy on the
boxing glove.

How to perform plastic surgery on your
mind.

Why you should quit waiting to feel
confident.

Why it's good to weigh up but not to
be weighed down by criticism.

How to carry out a success stock
take.

Having explored how other people can have a positive
impact on your levels of confidence, let's turn the spotlight
onto you and discover how you can become your own best
mate. To do so means taking charge of how you think
about your own strengths and weaknesses.

Here are some great insights and ideas to help you do
just that.

Seven 10 Percent Tips to Avoid Sabotaging Your Confidence

1   Accept that "flaws are us"

Your background, upbringing, culture, media and education can all communicate a message that on one level seems
both noble and desirable: "Be good. Do the best you can.
Aim to improve."

That seems fine, and I endorse those statements. But along
with them, perhaps unspoken or included in the small
print, are the following messages: "You're not good enough,
do more, you're not as good as ..."

It seems like a two-edged sword. For some people their
desire for self-improvement is born out of a sense of inadequacy and a belief that they're not OK. Sometimes we can
be left feeling that no matter what we do or what we
achieve, we'll never quite arrive.

Can you relate to that at all?

Perhaps that's what lies at the heart of a capitalist society. A need to create a need. And how can the need be met and the gap filled unless people become aware of it?

So, in an effort to meet this need and fill the gap, some people embark on a never-ending search to find a quick fix or a magic wand answer to their problems. They listen to the latest guru, who they place on a pedestal marked "hope". They buy their books, they attend their seminars, they listen to their CDs.

And they feel good.

Sometimes they feel very good.

And then slowly

over time

the good feelings

fade and

fade

until

a new fix

a new cure is presented to them.

And so the cycle continues and we all play the never-ending game called "How to feel good about yourself" while at the same time being bombarded with reasons on why we shouldn't.

And do you know what?

Deep down we know we will never win the game because no matter how hard we try

we fall short.

We may feel OK

for a time

but then something happens. And it's like we're having to start all over again.

The truth is ...

When you play the game 'Be Perfect', you will always end up on the losing team.

And the reason is that we've failed to admit to one simple truth. A truth that the media and many self-help books don't want us to realize.

We're flawed.

We all are.

And no matter what you do or how hard you try this fundamental fact remains.

You're not perfect.

And never will be.

And guess what?

That's OK.

It's OK not always to be OK. That doesn't mean that we don't need to improve, to work hard, to stretch ourselves. It's simply a recognition that part of what makes us human is our flaws and, accepting that as a package, we can be both flawed *and* fantastic.

Just three words: flawed and fantastic. But when we embrace and accept that description of ourselves, it can make a big difference to our self-esteem and confidence.

Pit Stop

∞ How often do you play the "Be Perfect" game?
∞ How do you feel about not being OK in some areas of your life?
∞ What's your main insight from seeing yourself as both flawed and fantastic?

2   Go easy on the boxing glove

In my talks I often highlight the role and impact of your inner critic. That's the voice inside your head that highlights your weaknesses and undermines your confidence. The voice may echo an angry parent, a critical teacher, a teasing classmate or a disappointed God.

As a visual illustration, I use a big red boxing glove that represents this voice and how you use it to beat yourself up.

Admittedly it might prove difficult to remove the glove permanently, but it's possible for the punches to become more like gentle taps that only take place occasionally. These "hits" can be seen as mild rebukes and reminders of when you may have fallen short, but they no longer need to be a barrage of incessant blows that can quite literally knock the confidence out of you.

At times we simply need to give ourselves the benefit of the doubt. It's said that charity begins at home – maybe compassion needs to start there as well. Agree?

However, please don't get me wrong. I'm not suggesting that you fall hopelessly and madly in love with yourself and turn a blind eye to your faults and failings. But I am suggesting that you take a kinder and more compassionate approach to how you see yourself. And in turn, you'll probably start to take a more compassionate view of others.

That sounds like common sense I'm sure, but how exactly do you do that? How can you be more compassionate with yourself? The next tip will give you some ideas. But first ...

Pit Stop

∞ What do you tend to beat yourself up about the most?
∞ How hard are the "punches"?
∞ Who do you know who needs to go easy on the boxing glove?
∞ Write down some ways in which you could help them.

3 Perform plastic surgery on your mind

There is tremendous power in what you say to yourself. Words can label you. They can both limit and liberate you. Either way, as we've already seen, they can have a profound long-term impact on you.

Just as people pay to have their outward appearance changed through a tummy tuck, a boob job or a face lift, you can perform your own form of plastic surgery. Your focus here is on your internal world and not your outward appearance. And you don't need to hire an expensive surgeon to do it.

Surgery often requires the cutting away of excess flesh or the injection of a substance such as botox. When performing surgery on your own mind, you're about to discover what language and phrases to "cut out" and what to inject in their place.

*Words to cut out of your vocabulary when
describing yourself*
I've covered some of these before when I explored the
negative beliefs we have about ourselves:

"I'm just a slob/lazy."
"I'll never be any good at ..."
"I'll never be able to change the way I am"
"I'm pathetic at ..."
"I'm always forgetting to ..."
"I'm always making that mistake."
"I'll never find anyone who loves me."

These phrases or any similar ones are now banned from
your vocabulary. For ever.

Inject the following phrases into your vocabulary
"I have the ability to improve from where I am now."
"I recognize I have some failings and I'm still an OK person."
"I'm making progress from where I was before."
"I'm taking steps to improve in the area of ..."
"I'm learning to learn from my mistakes."
"I'm taking action to improve my situation."
"I recognize and value the many qualities I have."
"I can handle this."
"I surprise myself with what I'm capable of achieving."

Plastic surgery is a radical step that can create a long-term
impact on your appearance (and many would say your
confidence as well). And to perform plastic surgery on your
mind, you need to do more than simply read a few words
on a page.

In some cases you may have to acknowledge that you could be guilty of *psychological self-harm* by the words you continually say to yourself and the thoughts and images you hold about yourself. Depending on how damaged you've become, you may need the help of an expert. I encourage you, if appropriate, to seek out the services of a therapist, particularly one who uses cognitive behavioural therapy (CBT) as a method to help their clients.

If such a radical step is not required – and in most cases it won't be – then reread the list of phrases to inject into your own vocabulary and choose three that you will write down and repeat to yourself at least ten times *every day* for the next 30 days. You can even write your own phrases – just make sure they're positive, empowering and say them (out loud if appropriate) like you believe it.

Here's a reminder of a phrase we looked at earlier, which really is an important insight to grasp.

The truth is ...

Beside God –
if you believe in God –
the most important
person you will ever
talk to is yourself.

Trust me, I'm being totally serious. It would be so easy to skip over that last exercise and do absolutely nothing. If that's the case then you're not being your own best mate.

This stuff works. Choose three phrases, that's all.

It might only make a 10 percent difference – but as we know that's all you need, because a small change in what you say to yourself can make a big difference to how you see yourself.

Go on then, what are you waiting for?

In fact, I challenge you to choose three phrases or create your own and email me with them. I promise I will acknowledge your email personally (my email address is Paul.McGee@theSUMOguy.com).

Right, that's the first three tips on how to avoid sabotaging your confidence: accept that "flaws are us," go easy on the boxing glove and perform plastic surgery on your mind. Now let's look at our fourth tip.

4   Get a grip of the wheel

Some people's life is like a car journey, except that they believe someone or something else is in the driving seat. That could be:

their boss
their parents
the government
fate
destiny

luck
their star sign

Whatever or whoever it is, it's not you. If that's the case, it's time for an honest sit down with yourself. It's time to spell out a few truths that may initially knock your confidence but ultimately will build and strengthen it.

If you believe you are where you are in life because of other people or luck or fate, you're deceiving yourself.

It's your car.

You have the keys.

Get a grip on the wheel and start driving it.

Quit the excuses.

No more hard luck stories.

No more blaming.

The destination of your life and how you get there is in your hands. If it's not, then you have allowed other people or circumstances to determine your destiny.

You might not have realized that before, but you do now – because I just told you.

Harsh?

Well, sometimes maybe a real friend needs to spell out the truth.

And sometimes the truth hurts.

But it's still the truth.

Maybe I'm being your Challenger.

Perhaps that's what you need right now.

Here's the score.

No one grew in self-confidence by placing their backside squarely and firmly in the passenger seat of their life.

And you won't either.

So change seats if you have to

and get both hands

on the wheel of your life.

Pit Stop

∞ Really take time to consider this question: Is there an area in your life where you're being the passenger?

∞ If so, what are you going to do about it?

∞ Who's the best person to help you: A Cheerleader? A Challenger? A Coach? A Confidant?

5 Quit waiting to *feel* confident

How did you learn to ride a bike? Did you visualize yourself riding the bike and then vividly imagine how you would feel once you had ridden it? Me neither.

Did you use positive affirmations to help yourself?

Probably not.

So what did you do?

Got on the bike and started to pedal.

Hopefully you had someone's help when you first started, but there came a point when you were riding that bike on your own. And it was at that moment that you truly became confident in your ability to ride a bike.

In other words, your feelings of confidence came

after,

not before,

your action.

That's an important lesson to learn.

You can often reduce your anxiety before an event (and we will look at how to do that in the next chapter), but you can't always expect to feel totally confident.

It just doesn't always work that way.

And that's OK.

So, is there something you don't feel particularly confident about at the moment?

Are you feeling nervous?

Fine.

Most people in your situation with your levels of ability and experience would probably feel the same.

Get over it.

The truth is ...

> If you're waiting for the right feeling before you take the right action – you could be waiting a long time.

Nerves are normal. So too is not always feeling totally confident before you do something.

That's a good thing.

Where's the challenges and thrills in life if you have to feel complete confidence before you do anything?

And here's something interesting.

It might even seem contradictory to what we've already been discussing.

Your thinking is important, but sometimes you can over-think!

You can analyze too much.

Sometimes you need to turn down the volume on your internal self-talk and just take action.

If you don't, there's a danger of paralysis by analysis.

Pit Stop

- ∞ Is there an action you've been putting off that you realize now is due to a lack of confidence?
- ∞ How uncomfortable do you feel about doing it? (On a scale of 1–10, where 10 is extremely uncomfortable.)
- ∞ In the light of what you've just read, what do you need to do now?
- ∞ So what are you waiting for?

The Personal Stuff

I've recently returned from a family holiday in Australia and New Zealand. While in New Zealand we visited Queenstown, which is known as the extreme sports capital of that country.

I don't do extreme sports. I'm not an adrenaline junkie. Gentle strolls along the beach or besides the river will do perfectly well for me, thanks. I don't even like theme parks as I suffer badly from motion sickness (if I'm ever a passenger in the back seat of your car you'll understand what I mean – and so will your car interior).

I once visited a children's theme park and, much to Helen's amusement, became quite unwell having gone on a roundabout with my then 3-year-old daughter. So I think it's fair to say that I am to extreme sports what Sumo wrestlers are to ballet – we're not particularly well matched.

But I'm writing a book on self-confidence and while I was in Queenstown I started thinking: "Am I destined to stay in my own cosy comfort zone in terms of physical activity for the rest of my life?"

If so, fine. But I wanted to challenge myself. Was there an area where I could stretch myself to grow in confidence? Yes there was. Indoor golf.

Just kidding.

It's actually quite hard to walk around Queenstown without being confronted with images in shops of people doing bungee jumps. Matt, my 16-year-old son, was quite tempted by the idea. I also felt tempted

to sit down in a pub and feast on some delicious potato wedges.

Then I made a decision. "Matt, if you want to do a bungee jump I'll do it as well."

Case closed. I just made a decision. I'm going for it.

I refuse to play safe all the time, and when people ask "What was Queenstown like?" to answer, "The potato wedges were to die for."

So that's what I did. August 1st 2009, a few days before my 45th birthday, I did my first ever bungee jump.

How did I deal with the anxiety of facing up to such an experience?

I quit waiting to feel confident.

I decided not to think about it too much.

I simply chose a reputable company

admired the views

and then 4 3 2 1

Bungee!

It was quite an experience. I treasure the photos (I actually did a fairly decent impression of Superman as I dived off the ledge). But do you know what was the most important lesson from the whole experience?

Here it is.

It's not what you achieve that's always the key issue, but how you feel about yourself once you've done it.

Re-read those words again. And make a decision to do something in your life where you stop the analyzing and decide to just take the action. I promise you, it will make a big difference.

And now for your sixth tip on how to avoid sabotaging your confidence.

6 Weigh up but don't be weighed down by criticism

Most people can find criticism challenging – especially if it's not given in a particularly helpful way. When that happens to you, you can choose one of the following responses:

∞ Ignore it – which is exactly what some people do.
∞ Dwell on it – an understandable response, particularly if your feelings have been hurt.
∞ Be defensive – again understandable, particularly if you feel the criticism is unjustified.
∞ Wait a while and then weigh it up – a response that might be easy to advise others to do, but not one that comes naturally to most of us, myself included.

It's that fourth response I want to focus on. It might not be easy to do, but it's a sign of emotional maturity and self-confidence when we're prepared to do it.

Here are some really useful questions to ask when weighing up criticism:

∞ How valid is that comment?
∞ What were the other person's motives for giving it?
∞ Can I understand their perspective?
∞ What part of the criticism (if any) could I agree with?
∞ Although natural, how is my defensive response helping this situation?
∞ Would I do anything differently next time?
∞ Am I prepared to thank my critic for their comments, even if I don't agree with them?

Pit Stop

∞ How do you usually respond to criticism? Which of the above questions could be really helpful for you to think about?
∞ Think about the last time you were criticized and work through the seven questions.
∞ Now that you've done so, what insights have you gained?

The Personal Stuff

150 people were crammed into a hotel on the outskirts of Rochdale. Although it was a challenging group, and despite my microphone not working, I thought that the first part of my masterclass on dealing with change had gone particularly well, all things considered.

At the break the head of diversity came to speak to me. "We've had one or two complaints about you, I'm afraid."

"Complaints?" I replied in a rather shocked and I'm sure slightly defensive tone.

"One or two women believe you've been racist and sexist in your language."

"Wow, I wasn't aware I was doing any of that. Can you be more specific?"

The head of diversity couldn't be more specific. She went back to the women to get more feedback. I offered to meet them to discuss their concerns in more detail.

They refused to meet me. They were unable to provide a specific example of any sexist language. However, they were quite clear about my racism.

"It's when you do your accents – they find that completely inappropriate."

Well, they had a point. I do use accents during my talk. One is in connection with a man called Gary from Northern Ireland, another is of a Geordie who wanted to buy a T-shirt from me, and the other is of a Russian-speaking dog (it's a long story!). I felt a mixture of surprise and also relief when I became clearer about the specific allegation of racism.

I weighed up the feedback. I guess if you're from Northern Ireland, Newcastle or Russia there is a possibility that you might feel I'm mocking your accent. I'm still not sure you would interpret it as racism, but I could (if I stretched my imagination far enough) appreciate that I may have caused some offence.

I guess their comments had some validity but I'm not sure what their motives were in giving it. Everyone else in the room seemed happy with the session – including the head of diversity. Thousands of other people have heard me do a similar talk and never complained.

I continued to weigh up the feedback on my drive home but in case you're wondering, I don't do anything different as a result of this criticism. I didn't ignore it, I weighed it up.

As far as I'm concerned, my impression of a Russian-speaking dog is staying in my presentation.

It's not easy to receive criticism. If you react defensively and dwell on it, you'll be weighed down by it. It can erode your confidence.

But criticism can also be a gift if you choose to weigh it up and learn from it. It could contain an insight that helps you achieve your goal. Sometimes it won't drain your confidence – it could actually boost it. A small nugget of truth could make all the difference.

7 Take a success stock take

Evolutionary biologists tell us that we're wired to remember our mistakes.

That's a good thing.

Repeat the same mistake twice and you might not be around long enough to have a third attempt.

It's a question of survival.

The problem is it seems whilst we're skilled at remembering our mistakes, faults and failings, we're less skilled at remembering our successes.

We discount them.

Perhaps take them for granted.

Our attitude being "I'm nothing special. It's no big deal."

After all, everyone can read, write, add up, drive a car, ride a bike, cook a meal.

Really?

Everyone?

Sometimes it's worthwhile doing a stock take of your successes. A stock take of your skills, qualities and attributes that you perhaps take for granted.

In doing so it's not to brag about how brilliant you are, or to convince yourself you're better than other people. It's just an honest assessment that acknowledges there's probably more to you than meets the eye.

And it's a great way to build your self-confidence.

How to avoid being limited by labels

Often part of the reason we fail to appreciate the wide range of skills and qualities we possess is due to the labels we use to describe ourselves. Understandably we tend to adopt a shorthand way of telling others what we do. So typically when we're asked the question "What do you do?" our answer is condensed into just a few words, e.g. I'm a student, I work in IT, I run my own business. One reason you may have bought this book is because you're currently unemployed. Yet using that word to describe yourself is only accurate in describing your current employment status. It does nothing to unpack the skills and experience you have acquired so far.

That's what the following exercise has been designed to do. It helps you to take a positive and honest look at yourself. By doing so it will boost your own personal confidence and should you find yourself looking for a job or going for promotion you'll find it invaluable.

Start first of all by not seeing yourself in the following narrow way:

Student	IT worker	Accountant
Sales representative	Unemployed	Business owner

It will be more helpful to look at yourself as a blend of skills rather than a single label:

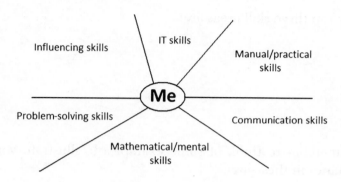

I have broken down your blend of skills into six areas, but there are numerous other ones. Now, there will be some that you're stronger in than others. That's fine. You'll find it helpful to think of an example for each category that illustrates your ability in that area. Why don't you quickly do that now? Go one step further and give yourself a rating out of 10 for each category. Clearly this is subjective, so also get someone who knows you well to also rate you, but without seeing your scores first.

	Your score out of 10	Your friend's score of you
IT skills	☐	☐
Influencing skills	☐	☐
Manual/practical skills	☐	☐
Communication skills	☐	☐
Mathematical/mental skills	☐	☐
Problem-solving skills	☐	☐

My top three skill areas are:

1
2
3

Remember to think of some examples to illustrate your abilities in these areas.

The above is intended as a starter. It's to get you thinking of yourself as more than just a label. A useful analogy would be that of a cake. It's made up of lots of ingredients many of which we don't think about when eating it. Perhaps the key ingredient you're missing from your cake is confidence. So one way to develop it would be to recognize the qualities and skills you already possess, but so far take for granted.

The truth is...

Some people dwell on their failures but skim over their successes.

Identifying your successes and achievements
Here are a few questions to help you assess and reflect upon your achievements:

1   What work achievement during the last three to five years has given you the most satisfaction?
2   What skills and qualities did you demonstrate in order to achieve this?
3   In what way did others benefit from this achievement?
4   What did you learn about yourself through this achievement?

Now repeat the exercise again but think of something you've achieved outside of work. It could be passing an exam, learning to drive, losing weight, quitting smoking, getting married, moving house. The list is endless. But take time out to not only acknowledge those achievements but also assess what skills and attributes you demonstrated in achieving them.

One way to structure your reflection is to use the S.T.A.R. method:

Situation

Target

Actions

Results

For example

Situation:	I found myself 10 kg overweight and lacking confidence and self worth
Target:	I decided I wanted to reach a target weight of 73 kg and set myself six weeks to lose 10 kg
Actions:	I decided to enlist the support of my wife and kids to help achieve my target. I reduced my intake of carbohydrates particularly after 6pm and also decided to go for a brisk 3 mile walk five times a week. I also joined a local slimming club
Results:	I managed to achieve my target weight within the given period. I learnt I do have the potential to succeed when I put my mind to it and get the support of others. As a result I feel my success has increased my self-confidence

Taking things further

Remember, the above exercises are simply meant to act as a catalyst and get you thinking about your strengths and qualities. They're designed to challenge the labels we use that can limit our own perception of ourselves. For a more in-depth look at this whole area I would recommend the work of Tom Rath and the Gallup organisation. Check out the book Strengths Finder 2.0 by Tom Rath or visit the website www.sf2. strengthsfinder.com.

in A Nutshell

Here are seven ways to become your own best mate (and avoid sabotaging your confidence):

1 Accept that "flaws are us" – Give up playing the "Be Perfect" game.

2 Go easy on the boxing glove – It's time to quit beating yourself up.

3 Perform plastic surgery on your mind – Take radical steps in regard to what you say to yourself.

4 Get a grip on the wheel – Get back in the driver's seat and take charge of your life.

5 Quit waiting to feel confident – Start taking action and the confidence will follow.

6 Weigh up but don't be weighed down by criticism – Evaluate feedback, don't evade it.

7 Take a success stock take. Be more aware of your skills, qualities and achievements.

Having discovered seven insights and ideas to help you be your own best mate, now let's explore some specific situations when self-confidence will be crucial to your success.

7 How to Shine When Your Neck's on the Line

You're about to discover

Why you
need to leave
your comfort zone
to achieve success.

How and why anxiety
affects you, and how to face it
and deal with it.

Two proven methods to calm down
and prevent anxiety escalating.

Six simple ways to shine when giving
a talk or presentation.

Two great insights on how to perform
at interviews, including the four
questions every interviewer wants
answers to.

Five ways to be cool, calm and
confident when dating other
people.

Has Your Comfort Zone Become a Prison?

Have you ever avoided a situation because it made you feel uncomfortable? Join the crowd, as I guess most of us have.

But here's the challenge:

if you want to succeed and achieve your goals, then there are going to be times when you've simply got to move out of your comfort zone. And that's not easy to do. The very thought can create anxiety.

And what's the outcome? When you need to be at your best you often feel at your worst.

Painful, eh?

So what's the way forward?

Stay in your comfort zone?

Continual avoidance?

Or

face up to your fear and reap the rewards?

At the end of the day ask yourself this question: "Where do life's opportunities lie? Inside or outside my comfort zone?"

Moving out of your comfort zone can be scary business.

It can be risky.

That's why many people don't do it.

But if you do decide to step out, you need to find ways to reduce your anxiety and build up your confidence. And that's what this chapter's about.

We're going to explore practical ways to help you shine during three experiences that most people would probably not have top of their "things I always feel confident about doing" list. Here they are:

∞ Public speaking or making a presentation
∞ Job interviews
∞ Asking someone on a date

Each has the potential to catapult you to the next level of success – equally, each could be featured in the book *My Worst Ever Life Experiences*.

However, before we do, let's explore why we often hear about other people's bad experiences and how this bad news feeds our fears, distorts reality and increases our anxiety.

The Reason Bad News Spreads so Fast

Remember the good times? Remember hearing about how your friend's job interview went really well, or recall how your colleague's sales presentation went brilliantly? Or what about the time when you went into an exam feeling confident and you felt totally in the zone when you answered the questions? Or the time your friend went on a blind date and they both fancied each other?

Remember?

Hardly.

You see, according to a study on psychological science our brains tend to fixate on bad memories. How do they know that? The study found that when we hear about an awful event, the part of the brain that processes emotions lights up far more than when we experience a neutral or positive event. This imprints heavily on our memory, hence we have the ability to remember and recall awful events.

Now here's the interesting thing. It's not that these negative events occur more often than positive ones – it's simply that we recollect them more easily and start to tell other people about them.

That's why most people have heard a story about the date or interviewer from hell or the time someone dried up while speaking in public. Because we've heard the stories, we trick ourselves into believing that these things happen more often than they actually do.

Why is that the case? There may be an evolutionary explanation – we are wired to remember threats rather than focus on or recall treats. It's a matter of survival.

Since one of the main functions of the brain is to keep us alive, it's particularly interested in helping us avoid potentially threatening situations. That's why we're wired to react with the fight or flight response in situations where the brain *perceives* a challenge to our survival.

This worked particularly well on the plains of the African Savannah when as part of a nomadic tribe you walk straight into the path of a sabre-toothed tiger. (OK, I realize they'd probably died out by the time humans were walking the planet, but you get my drift.) You're either going to fight it or run like crazy.

But there's a problem: your brain still thinks you're living in the land of sabre-toothed tigers. So it's rather sensitive to stimuli or situations it perceives (there's that word again) as threatening – even if the threat is psychological, not physical.

And one of the biggest and often most traumatic psychological threats that people face is rejection. That's why putting yourself in a position where there's a chance you could be rejected increases your stress levels.

Why You're Stressed When You Need to Shine

In order to deal with a threat your brain secretes various chemicals – namely adrenaline and cortisol – to prepare you for battle.

There are no tigers.

There might not even be any real threat

but the brain's not taking any chances.

It doesn't hold an internal board meeting to discuss the pros and cons of taking action. It reacts. Sometimes inappropriately.

Before you know it, you're fleeing or fighting. Occasionally, you're freezing – your body seems to temporarily shut down and you find it almost impossible to access the rational part of your brain.

Chemicals are racing round your body.

Your heart is beating faster.

Your pupils are dilating.

Your palms are sweating.

Your throat is dry.

And the reason?

Sabre-toothed tiger?

No.

You've just been asked to do a two-minute welcome at the annual staff conference – to over 500 people.

You're waiting to attend your interview panel.

You've just spotted an extremely attractive person at the bar.

And you need to shine when you feel most stressed.

Ever felt that way?

OK, but hang on a minute. You need to remember this:

The truth is ...

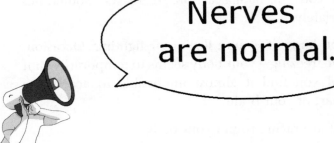

Nerves are normal.

Let's get one thing straight,

you don't want to eliminate your nerves.

Feeling confident does not mean that you never feel nerves.
Confidence comes from controlling your nerves rather than
them controlling you. As a friend of mine once said, "You
can't get rid of the butterflies, but you can teach them to fly
in formation."

That's really important to remember.

Nerves is simply a word you use to describe a set of feelings
you're experiencing internally that's been triggered by
your at times rather overprotective brain. In a different
context, you may actually describe those same feelings as
excitement (for instance getting married, or doing a bungee
jump – although preferably not at the same time).

Your brain recognizes that you need to be at your best. It
tries to help you by increasing your levels of concentration
and putting you in a high state of arousal. That's why those
chemicals are released and you experience certain physical
symptoms.

The problems occur when arousal leads to anxiety – rather
than preparing you to perform at your best, you're now
emotionally and physically at your worst.

Ever had that experience?

At an interview?

Giving a talk?

On a date?

The following will help in whatever situation you're in.

Don't Flee from Your Anxiety, Face Up to It

When you're vaccinated you receive a weakened version of the micro-organism that threatens you. In other words, you receive a small dose of the stuff that could harm you. In many ways, gradual exposure to the thing you fear works in the same way.

That's why sometimes the only way to deal with your fears or anxieties is to be prepared to face up to them.

Feeling anxious is not the problem. The problem occurs when you allow the anxiety to overwhelm you and it prevents you from being at your best.

You see, being over-anxious causes you to *exaggerate* the negative impact of an event or the likelihood of that event occurring.

You lose perspective.

It also causes you to *underestimate* your ability to deal with a situation.

And anxiety can escalate into fear.

Fear can cripple you.

It disables you. It can imprison you.

Depressed yet?

But now for the good news.

It doesn't have to be that way.

How to Calm Down

The following exercise will be a great help if you do it. (You will find it beneficial to say the statements out loud to yourself in a calm and quiet tone of voice.) I sometimes refer to it as the F.A.T. method.

Step 1 Feel your anxious feelings
"I'm experiencing feelings of anxiety at the moment."

Step 2 Accept them
"I recognize this anxiety has been triggered because I perceive some kind of threat or challenge to myself or loved ones."

Step 3 Thank them
"I'm grateful my brain wants to protect me. I now use my internal resources to deal calmly and appropriately with the situation."

Here's another exercise you may find helpful. It's a visualization exercise and one to do with your eyes shut.

Imagine a train arriving at a station. Each carriage of the train represents your thoughts – or your train of thoughts. Each carriage also represents a particular emotion or feeling.

Imagine yourself on the platform. As the train stops the carriage in front of you is marked "Anxiety."

You look into the carriage. There's definitely anxiety in there.

The doors open. You remain on the platform.

The doors close. The train departs.

Watch the train as it pulls out of the station. Watch as you see anxiety leaving. Watch until you can no longer see the train.

Remind yourself:

"I feel feelings – but I am not my feelings."

"I think thoughts – but I am not my thoughts."

The truth is ...

It's OK to have the feelings, but you don't need to hold onto them.

Deep relaxation techniques are also a great strategy to alleviate anxiety – especially if you can find a couch, a set of headphones and your latest CD of whale sounds from the Antarctic.

Joking apart, all the above strategies will help, particularly if you can find the time and place to relax. But what if you can't?

Here are some further practical ways to help you shine when your neck's on the line. Let's explore the three situations separately.

Petrified of Public Speaking?

Actually, you're probably not petrified. You just tell yourself you are. In fact, there's some ridiculous research purporting to the fact that many people would rather die than speak in public.

Really?

So you would rather end your life now, leave your kids without a mother or father, never again experience the thrill of sex, marvel at a sunset, swim in the sea, feast on good food – you would rather miss out on all that than speak in public?

Yeah, right.

So let's put that myth where it belongs – in the bin. It makes a nice title for a magazine article or book, but there's one problem.

It's a lie.

You may be nervous. You may even say you're petrified, but you're not willing to die in order to avoid doing it, are you?

Get real.

So what can you do to be at your best when you've got to present or speak in public? Here are some simple but great ways to calm your nerves and wow your audience.

Six 10 Percent Tips For Public Speaking

1   Turn the spotlight onto your audience

Much of your anxiety when speaking occurs because you turn your focus and nervous energy inwards. You turn the spotlight onto yourself and the questions you ask yourself only escalate your anxiety:

"What will people think of me?"
"What if I forget my words?"
"What if I get asked some awkward questions?"
"What if I run out of time?"
"What if I dry up?"

Not exactly the most positive and empowering questions, are they? And they're all focusing on you.

However, if you turn your attention and energy onto your audience and their needs, you might start asking some different questions:

"How can I make this talk relevant to my audience?"
"How can I best engage them?"
"What are their needs at the moment?"
"What's going on in their world?"
"If there was one key message I wanted to leave them with, what would it be?"

Suddenly it's your audience who's in the spotlight, not you.

The truth is ...

When you think more about others, you stress less about yourself.

2   Say less, achieve more

Most people try to give too much information to their audience. Actually, the value lies not in how much you say, but in what you say and how you say it. It's about the quality of the information, not the quantity.

People are being bombarded with information. It can be overwhelming. They'll only retain a small percentage of your content – unless, that is, you say less but expand more.

For example, in a 30-minute talk or presentation it's more effective to cover three main points and use examples and illustrations to expand on each one than to try to cover nine or ten points. Your goal is to make your message memorable – and using too many facts achieves the exact opposite.

3   Put PowerPoint in its place

I use slides in my presentations, I'm not part of the anti-PowerPoint brigade – I just recognize that it's possible to rely too much on them, and when you do use them, to use them badly.

Slides are supposed to enhance your presentation. They're part of your act but they're not meant to take centre stage – they're part of the supporting cast.

So quit hiding behind them. If you do, you're just part of the scenery and could be seen as irrelevant.

There are lots of tips that you can easily access about the do's and don'ts of PowerPoint or similar packages. A particularly amusing but helpful piece about the subject can be found on www.youtube.com. Type in Don McMillan and view "How NOT to use PowerPoint."

4   Say it with props

If you're going to shine you need to be noticed and remembered. A great way to do both and increase the impact of your talk is to use props. Some of the props I use include tee-shirts, a broken record, a beachball and a boxing glove (if you want to see an example of how I use my props, go to www.TheSumoGuy.com).

5   Stories sell

If you want to appeal to people's emotions as well as their intellect, then tell stories. We're never persuaded to take an action or adopt a particular point of view based purely on a rational, logical argument.

We're emotional. We connect with things we can relate to. We connect to the experiences of others that in some way echo our own.

That's not a new discovery. Just look at religious leaders from the past. When Jesus was asked "Who is my neighbour?" what did he do? Draw a pie chart? Get a map and divide the country into areas?

No. He told the story of the Good Samaritan. And 2,000 years later people still know it. It's packed with insight, intrigue and emotion – just like the stories of other religious leaders and philosophers such as Jean Paul Sartre who communicated some profound insights through his book *Nausea* and used the story as a way to express his philosophical message. Political figures like Dr. Martin Luther King Jnr, Bill Clinton and Tony Blair all used stories to engage their audience and to strengthen the bond between them and their listeners.

Stories help us connect with others. They arouse emotions within people. (For more information on the art of telling stories, go to www.fripp.com and www.dougstevenson. com)

Not only can stories be powerful and memorable, they're also easier for you to remember than a stack of facts and figures. That alone can increase your confidence, as well as giving you a brilliant opportunity to dazzle your audience.

6 Avoid the hearse, go and rehearse

It's possible to die on stage. I know. I've seen it.

On one occasion I even experienced it.

Let me tell you, it's not a great experience attending your own speaking funeral.

As for why this happens, there could be several reasons: inappropriate humour, a patronizing approach or a group who were unhappy before you started speaking. (I was once asked to deliver a talk on delivering a great service – minutes after most of the group learnt they were to be made redundant.)

But one factor contributing to why you might die is simply due to a lack of preparation on your part.

You didn't rehearse.

You weren't sure of your material.

You didn't check out the technology.

You didn't prepare enough – because deep down you didn't care enough.

The truth is ...

Sometimes it's not anxiety that kills a great performance - it's complacency.

Tiger Woods still practices his golf. In fact, all the true top performers practice. Practice breeds confidence. It helps people perform at their best.

You don't want to die – you want to shine.

So quit winging it and start practicing.

Practice not only what to say but how you say it.

You'll find that there are hundreds of articles and books, CDs and DVDs on how to be a better speaker. The point to remember is that it's not down to some innate mystical talent that you're born with. OK, some people do seem more naturally inclined to shine as speakers, but the gloss soon fades if they don't develop their skills.

When you apply the right polish, which typically comes in the form of practice and learning the skills of speaking, you'll be surprised at how much your confidence grows.

I run my own two-day workshop on presentation and speaking skills. It's not for the faint-hearted and neither is it a basic introduction. For more information email sumo@ paulmcgee.com.

Here are those six ideas again:

∞ Turn the spotlight onto your audience.
∞ Say less, achieve more.
∞ Put PowerPoint in its place.
∞ Say it with props.
∞ Stories sell.
∞ Avoid the hearse, go and rehearse.

Pit Stop

∞ Go back over the list of six ideas. Choose two to enhance your next talk or presentation.
∞ Think of the benefits that you and your audience will gain from using these ideas.
∞ Which ones will you pass on to someone else as a way to improve their next presentation?

Those are a few ideas about speaking, now let's explore another area that can be your downfall or your springboard to success.

Inspired at Interviews?

Whether it's going for a promotion or applying for a job externally, at some stage of the process you're going to sit down and be interviewed. It could be on a one-to-one basis or perhaps to a panel, but either way, you're definitely centre stage.

And the heat is on.

You may have passed the tests, played the games and done the role plays. The tough bit may feel like it's over, but all could be won or lost at the interview.

Here are some great ways to increase the chances of putting yourself in the best possible light.

Two 10 Percent Tips For Job Interviews

1   If you care then prepare

I've been asked some bizarre questions in interviews. For example, "If you were God, what would be an ideal night's television for you?" I resisted saying *Songs of Praise.*

Carrying on the religious theme, the same interviewer, having noted that I went to church, enquired, "Tell me what you think Jesus meant when he cried out on the cross 'My God, my God, why have you forsaken me?'"

I was applying for a job in human resources. Crucifixion was not in the job description.

Another bizarre incident I heard about involved a student who arrived for an interview only to be confronted by the interviewer sitting reading a newspaper and demanding in an aggressive manner: "Grab my attention." The story goes that the student set light to the newspaper in order to do so!

But despite the rather bizarre approach of some interviewers, good ones actually only want to find out the answers to four main questions:

∞ Can you do the job?
∞ Will you fit into the company's culture?
∞ Why do you want to work here?
∞ How much will you work for?

While that sounds straightforward enough there are actually 101 ways to ask each of those questions. (Although it's worth noting that not all interviewers will recognize that when you cut to the chase, there are really only four questions they need answers to). When you realize this it can demystify the whole experience.

Now you're clearer on what the interviewer(s) wants to achieve from this meeting, you can start to prepare some answers. Ideally the interview will then simply be a two-way exchange of information rather than a game of chess where you're trying to outwit your opponent.

And unless you're unfortunate enough to be interviewed by a power-obsessed masochist with a hidden agenda (and to be fair, I have come across a couple), most interviewers would be thrilled if you're the right candidate.

A good interviewer provides you with the opportunity to shine – but you might not realize that they're doing so. Questions such as the following are designed to help you sell yourself:

"Tell me more about yourself."
"What's an achievement you're particularly proud of?"
"Why do you think you're the right person for the job?"
"What questions do you have for us?"

Just like speaking in public, it's possible to die in an interview. Sometimes it's simply because a question stumps you, but invariably it's due to your lack of preparation.

The truth is ...

Always believing
you can 'wing it' is
not a sign of confidence
- it's an example
of arrogance.

So let's be clear. This might be a book about confidence, but the fact is that self-belief and feeling confident are not enough – unless you've done the preparation.

There are lots of people going for interviews full of self-confidence. But a good interviewer is keen to know what that confidence is based on – when you scratch the surface, what's really there? That's why you should expect challenging and probing questions.

Arrogance will undermine you and alienate you from the interviewer, so you've got to know your stuff. You've got to justify, with examples, your achievements. You have to present yourself in the best possible light. And that's why preparation before the interview is so important.

That leads us nicely on to our next point.

2 Shining without sinning

When you're going for a job – unless it's one that no one else wants: Roy Keane's yoga teacher, for instance – you have to see *yourself* as a product. You're the product and you've got to sell yourself.

And no matter what position you're applying for, you have to see yourself as a salesperson. (How can you get people to "buy you" unless you sell yourself?)

Now, that thought may do little to inspire you.

In fact, you may recoil in disgust at the very idea.

Why?

Possibly because you have a warped, distorted and, dare I say it, inaccurate perception of what makes a great salesperson.

Here are some common misconceptions about what makes a great salesperson:

∞ Must have the gift of the gab
∞ Pushy
∞ Arrogant
∞ Won't take no for an answer
∞ Money driven
∞ In love with themselves
∞ A liar

(And no, I wasn't describing your ex-partner.)

Those may be accurate statements to describe *some* sales-people, but the majority of successful ones aren't like the above (honest, they're not).

I've been running my own business for over 18 years. To succeed, I've needed to sell: to sell my ideas and to sell myself. I've had to influence and persuade people that I am worth their investment.

If you ask me what I do, I won't answer "I'm a salesman." But if you ask me what skills are required to succeed in business, then selling is right up there at the top of the list.

The truth is ...

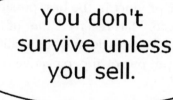

You don't survive unless you sell.

And you won't succeed at an interview unless you sell yourself effectively and appropriately. So let's explore some of the qualities that salespeople need to succeed:

∞ *Belief in the product.* You have to believe in the value of what you're selling and how it will help your customers.
∞ *Know your stuff* about the product, the market and the customer.

∞ *Smart persistence.* Rejection comes as a part of the job. But you need to know when to persist and when to move on – hence smart persistence.

∞ *Self-respect.* Your relationship with yourself and how much self-respect you have will influence your relationships with others and the respect you show in how you communicate with them.

∞ *Motivation.* You need this particularly in challenging times. Recognize that depending on your own personality or current circumstances, different factors will motivate you. That might be money, but often a more powerful motivating factor is recognition.

∞ *The ability to spin.* Clearly, you want to present yourself and your product in the best possible light. The phrase "spin doctor" has received a lot of negative press. But I live in the real world and the reality is that we all spin – we all put our own perspective on the truth.

Pit Stop

∞ List three of your personal qualities and think of a specific example to illustrate each one.

∞ Identify an achievement you're particularly proud of. What does that success say about you?

∞ In what way will your answers to the two questions above benefit an employer?

So when does shining become sinning?

∞ When we tell a blatant lie.

∞ When we cannot back up our achievements with any examples.

∞ When we "waffle".
∞ When we elevate ourselves by putting others down.
∞ When we rely on arrogance rather than ability.

(Examples of the above have been consistently demonstrated by contestants on the hit British TV series *The Apprentice*.)

So shine in your interviews by:

∞ Researching the company, it's markets and it's competitors.
∞ Researching yourself and listing not only your strengths and qualities, but examples of each. (It's critical that you do this.)
∞ Respecting yourself for who you are, not just what you do.
∞ Recognizing that setbacks are also stepping stones to success. (A friend of mine kept all his job application rejections in a folder marked "The they've missed out on me file.")
∞ Understanding that your shining might threaten some people. That's their problem, not yours – but if they're the interviewer, it may be the reason you don't get the job.
∞ Always seeking to invest in yourself and your development. (The American philosopher Jim Rohn says, "Work hard on your job, but work harder on yourself.")

To end this section on interviews, remember that the truth is ...

> The person who gets hired is not necessarily the person who can do the job the best, but the one who knows the most about how to get hired.

For further information you may want to read my book *How to Write a C.V. that Really Works*, which includes a section on job interviews. I have also listed some other helpful books on this topic in the More Stuff That Will Help section at the end of the book.

Pit Stop

∞ What's the biggest mistake you've ever made at an interview?
∞ What did you learn from the experience?
∞ Apart from job interviews, where else do you need to see yourself as a salesperson?

So we've learnt how to shine when speaking in public and at interviews. Now on to the final section of this chapter: asking someone on a date.

A Date with Destiny?

There's a popular book on the subject of dating called *The Game*. And whether we like it or not, dating is a game.

Other animals have their rituals – peacocks display their plumage, for instance. But when it comes to close encounters of the romantic kind, the only thing some people display is a shed load of ignorance.

Whether you're new to dating or returning to the scene after a relationship break-up, there are a number of ways to prevent the experience becoming a disaster. (And even if you've no intentions of ever going on a date, you're still about to discover lots of ideas that will help you in a variety of social situations.)

I've written a book on relationships and I've been interviewed by the media on the art of dating, but for this section of the book I'm also grateful to my brother Andy, who at the time of writing is single. His insights come from both experience and his study of this fascinating subject. Like the rest of this book this section contains a western cultural bias, but whatever your culture, I promise there are some ideas and insights to help you shine.

Five 10 Percent Tips For Dating

1   Perspective pays

Perhaps the main reason for anxiety when it comes to dating is the pressure we put ourselves under:

"What if they say no?"
"What if she doesn't like me?"
"What if she's the one?"

Relax.

Your primitive brain is currently in the driving seat and as things stand, believes that it may have spotted a potential mate. As a result, it's highly focused and completely blind to all other possible mates.

It also believes it's in competition with other predators who are seeking the same prize.

You feel a surge in adrenaline.

The pressure is on.

Or is it?

I appreciate that trying to be logical when it comes to physical attraction is a bit like giving a toddler their favourite sweets and saying: "Save them for later."

It's not easy.

But on the other hand, it's not impossible.

So let's apply a little logic and not allow our primitive brain to completely hijack our thought processes.

Let's imagine you find someone especially attractive and want to pursue your interest further. Remember, your aim in approaching the other person is not to ask for their hand in marriage. (If it is, I feel you've missed a few stages in the process.)

Neither are you asking them to commit to a romantic relationship.

Remind yourself that what you are in fact saying is, "If I'm honest, I find myself sufficiently attracted to you that I'd like to spend a little more time getting to know you."

And that's it.

Your neck's not really on the line. Take the heat off yourself. You're taking the first step. Depending on the other person's response, it might be the first step on the road to nowhere.

But maybe it's the first step of a relationship journey that could lead to a long-term commitment. Who knows?

And that's the point. Who knows? No one.

That is, until you decide to take the first step.

And if they say no?

I'm not going to say "don't take it personally" – because you will. And if you had built up your expectations about where this relationship might end up, then you're going to be disappointed.

For a while.

But guess what?

Nothing has changed. This person wasn't in your life previously and they're still not in your life now. There are still several million possible options out there.

So get things into perspective.

2 Let's do coffee

Given the need to apply a little *less* pressure to yourself when you're asking someone on a date, don't suggest going for dinner.

First, it's expensive – unless you choose somewhere really cheap, and that's clearly not sending the right message.

Secondly, it's long.

It's a long time to be together, particularly if things are not going well. So unless you skip starters and desserts, most dinner dates will usually be in excess of 90 minutes. That's like sitting through an entire football match. And believe me, that can seem an awfully long time if things aren't going well (just ask any Bradford City supporter).

Thirdly, dinner dates aren't the best way to put people at ease:

"Do I talk with my mouth full?"
"Which spoon do I use?"
"I can't believe the price of their fish and chips."
"I don't understand half the menu."

So do coffee instead. It's cheap – compared to a three-course meal anyway. It doesn't have to take too long, but if things are going well you can always have a second cuppa.

There's also less need for etiquette. There aren't many ways to create a bad impression when drinking coffee (but don't slurp and do make sure your cappuccino doesn't leave you with a frothy moustache, which in all honesty isn't an attractive trait in women).

Finally it's a relaxing environment, where you're more likely to be yourself and feel less pressure than on a more formal date.

The Personal Stuff

Where you go on a date can say a lot about you as a person. My dad used to take my mum round graveyards – he was fascinated by what was written on gravestones. Despite that, they still married.

I took my wife Helen to see my local football team. The game was not too absorbing, but at least it proved her love for me.

I had less success with a girl called Bernadette. I took her to the cinema to see the film *Scum*. It stars a young Ray Winston and graphically portrays life in borstal (a young offenders' institute). It ends with a gang rape scene and the victim committing suicide.

That was the last time I saw Bernadette. There's no pleasing some people.

When I was a student I met a woman called Ruth who was a singer in a band by night, but worked in a bakery by day. Over time it became clear that our eye contact was increasing and our smiles broadening as I checked out the meat and potato pies.

She invited me over for dinner. I was thrilled. For a student any offer of a free meal was gratefully received and the bonus was I might get a snog thrown in as well.

I was disappointed. My meal (if you can call it that) consisted of a Fray Bentos chicken and ham pancake and a tin of cheap baked beans. I wasn't impressed. I regretted bringing her flowers. There was no snog either.

A year later we married.

We didn't really – I made that last bit up.

Pit Stop

∞ Can you remember your first date? How were you feeling beforehand?
∞ Have you ever had a dating disaster?
∞ What did you learn from the experience?

3   Dress with care

Let's get one thing clear, "never judge a book by its cover" has to be one of the worst pieces of advice ever given when it comes to dating.

It's also potentially dangerous.

We're hard-wired to make snap decisions about people. At a very basic level, the question we're always asking when we encounter someone for the first time is

"friend or foe?"

These snap decisions are not always right (and our prejudices and culture influence them). But we can't ignore them.

The truth is ...

If you want them to read the content, make sure the cover is appealing.

Here are some actions to take:

∞ Do you have access to a full-length mirror? If not, get one.
∞ Take a look at your wardrobe. Is it time to dump some of the old favourites that looked really good on you – ten years ago?

∞ Get some feedback from a good but honest friend or colleague about what you wear.

∞ Ignore any advice your mother gives you about your clothes.

∞ Become more conscious of your clothing and what it says about you.

∞ Watch some fashion makeover programmes – they really can provide good, practical and often cheap advice.

I appreciate this may all sound superficial, but we're dealing with how the world is, not how you want it to be. Making an effort with your appearance invariably makes you feel better about yourself, which leads to increased self-confidence.

However, a word of warning. Remember that you're meeting for coffee – over-dress for the occasion and you're sending the wrong message.

The truth is ...

> You want to make an effort without appearing to have made too much of an effort.

That's great advice for a first informal date, although clearly you need to raise the stakes at more formal gatherings.

And if the person pays you a compliment about what you're wearing, *don't* reply with any of the following:

"Oh, I got them really cheap in a sale."
"Oh this old thing – I've had it for ages."
"I'm not sure, I think it makes my boobs look big" (definitely one to avoid if you're a man).

If someone pays you a compliment, two words will suffice: "Thank you."

In fact, being able to receive a compliment is in itself a sign of confidence.

4 Be remembered – for all the right reasons

I can think of plenty of ways to be remembered for all the wrong reasons:

∞ Bad breath.
∞ Turning up late.
∞ Body odour.
∞ Talking about ex-partners.
∞ Never asking about the other person.
∞ Moaning about your health or life in general.

(Have you ever met or dated anyone who's exhibited any of the above?)

So how can you stand out from the crowd without appearing proud? Here are two ways.

Be interested

Make sure you show plenty of interest in the other person. Listening isn't about waiting for your turn to talk. It's a brilliant opportunity to show the other person respect as well as help you discover more about them.

But avoid the Spanish Inquisition. You're trying to establish a connection, not explore deep-seated personal issues. It's a date, not a therapy session.

If the conversation starts getting heavy and you sense you're moving into deep unchartered waters, bring things back to shallow water by changing the subject. It might help to have a couple of questions prepared in advance to drop into the conversation at an appropriate time:

∞ Who would you most like to have a one-to-one with (living or dead)?
∞ Complete the phrase "not a lot of people know this but ..." (something interesting or memorable about you that not a lot of people know).

Whichever questions you use, make sure that you have some. There's nothing more damaging to your confidence than long periods of uncomfortable silence.

Be interesting

That can be a challenge to some people. Having the attitude "But I can't think of anything interesting about me" may explain the reason for your single status.

Don't worry if you don't have any particular hobbies – there's bound to be something you do in life that's interesting and you're not too embarrassed to admit to.

But do give some thought to how you talk about yourself and your interests. (Just as you would at a job interview – although hopefully this is a less formal experience.)

For instance, as you may have gathered by now I enjoy football. But if I was on a date and was asked what I enjoy, I could say either of the following:

∞ "I enjoy football." If the other person doesn't like football, that could be the end of the conversation.
∞ "I love football. There's nothing to compare to going to a live match. Have you ever been in a stadium full of tens of thousands of passionate people? It's amazing. I love the atmosphere. The tension. The whole build-up to the game. Football for me isn't just about watching 22 men kick around a bag of wind. It's so much more. It's about meeting up with my mates, the banter, the expectation of success. I love the whole experience. Not just the 90 minutes." (Aren't you impressed with how exciting I managed to make going to see Bradford City sound?)

That might sound over the top, but it's up to you to communicate about yourself in an engaging way. Even if the other person doesn't share your interest, they're still likely to be impressed. Who wants to spend time with someone lacking in any passion for life?

Make sure that you apply the same strategy when talking about your work. Let me elaborate.

Let's imagine you're in a profession that some people, rightly or wrongly, think is fairly boring – you're an accountant. How about describing what you do in a more intriguing way?

For instance, you could say: "I'm in the most misunderstood profession in the world. People pay me to save them money, while staying on the right side of the law."

Or you could just say, "I'm an accountant."

The choice is yours.

Remember, the person opposite you is deciding whether they want to see you again. They're deciding whether they want to spend more time in your company. They're judging you by the cover. And that isn't just simply based on what you look like, but also how you come across as a person. If the chapter titles don't look interesting, don't expect them to read further.

The bottom line?

You might not get a second chance to create a first impression.

This is your time to shine. Don't waste it.

The truth is ...

It's dangerous to rely on your natural wit and charm - particularly when you don't possess any.

Pit Stop

∞ On a scale of 1–10, how good are you at showing genuine interest in other people?

∞ What would be the benefits to you if you talked a little less and listened a little more?

∞ Think about your work and interests. How could you describe them in a more engaging or intriguing way?

∞ Write down the top three most interesting things about yourself.

In terms of your date with destiny, let's remind ourselves of the ten percent tips we've looked at so far:

∞ Perspective pays.
∞ Let's do coffee.
∞ Dress with care.
∞ Be remembered – for all the right reasons.

Here's your fifth and final one.

5 Rejections are reality

It's rare to find anyone who hasn't experienced some form of rejection. So when it happens to you, take some comfort in the fact that you're sharing in a universal experience.

The key is not whether it happens or not, but how to respond when it does.

First, be aware that one reason for your rejection could be down to your level of confidence – you may be perceived as having too much.

The truth is ...

> A touch of nerves and a little self-deprecation can be quite appealing in small doses. Displaying too much self-confidence can be quite intimidating.

Secondly, rejection presents you with an opportunity. Now that could be an opportunity to purchase a voodoo doll and a set of pins, or to book a large hall for your pity party.

Or it could also be a time for some honest reflection.

The value of this reflection depends on whether it's spent with your inner critic or your inner coach. (Remember, we looked at this in the chapter "How to be your own best mate.") Typically, the emotional and rather loud voice of the inner critic kicks in initially:

"I'm fat."
"I'm ugly."
"I'm destined to remain single."

You might be surprised to hear that such comments are designed to protect you from further rejection. If you believe you're fat, ugly and destined to remain single, you're unlikely to put yourself in a position where you're going to be rejected again.

And if you buy into that belief, you'll probably remain

unhappy and unfulfilled

for the rest of your life.

So how about you sit down and have a little chat with your inner coach instead?

Once the initial emotions of rejection have subsided (I'm not suggesting they will disappear), you may want to reflect on the following:

∞ Was I perhaps a little hasty in asking that person on a date?
∞ Would I use the same approach when meeting someone else for the first time? (Perhaps showing them your tattoo on your left buttock was construed as being a little too forward?)
∞ What went well in my interaction with that person?

∞ What would I do differently next time? (Keep your trousers on perhaps?)

And if the rejection comes after a few dates:

∞ What have I learnt about myself from this experience?
∞ Were we really compatible?
∞ In what way might I have contributed to the relationship ending?
∞ What did I enjoy about the relationship?
∞ What lessons can I take from this experience into my next relationship?

The truth is ...

> Experience is not a great teacher. It's only a great teacher when you choose to learn from it. That's why people keep repeating the same mistakes.

Pit Stop

Let me be your challenger for a moment.

∞ If you keep making the same relationship mistakes, what are you trying to prove?
∞ What are the payoffs for you in repeating the same mistakes? Don't try to convince yourself that there aren't any, because there are.
∞ What have you learnt about yourself from relationships with others?

To explore any questions raised in this Pit Stop, you might find it useful to read about the first SUMO principle, "Change your T-shirt." There are details about my book in "the 'More Stuff That Will Help Section'."

The truth is ...

> Remember, rejection can go two ways. It can make you better or it can leave you bitter.

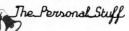

The Personal Stuff

This is Andy's story:

When I was at university doing a second degree, I split up from a long-term relationship. Because we'd been partners for seven years, I was completely out of my depth when it came to dating women. My first relationship after the split was with someone I'd prefer to refer to as the Peroxide Blonde (hey, who says I'm bitter?). Peroxide was not the most reliable of women. We'd plan to meet up and she'd fail to show up – often without phoning to let me know. Other times she would cancel at the last minute. In short, she didn't respect my time, which I guess is another way of saying she didn't respect me.

In hindsight I realized I liked her more than she liked me. So instead of pulling her up on her behaviour, I let it go, hoping that things would get better. They didn't.

My feelings for her grew more intense. Her respect for me nose-dived.

I got hurt. Big time.

But I've learnt from the experience. I asked myself what I would do differently next time, faced with similar behaviour.

I decided that if a similar situation ever arose again, I would either mention it and give the person a chance to show me it was merely a one-off, or I would finish the relationship straight away. I wasn't going to allow myself to become carried away again by the excitement and emotions that accompany the first few weeks and months of a new relationship with someone who was unreliable.

I think it's far better to decide in advance what you want and what you're prepared to live with in a relationship, rather than to try to work it out while you're forming intense feelings for someone. If you don't do this, you are much more liable to be hurt and have your confidence undermined, for two reasons. First, you show you don't respect yourself because you tolerate behaviour you are not happy with. That makes it harder for the other person to respect you.

Secondly, you are far more likely to mention something when your emotions are running high, and this can be disastrous. I fell into that trap, thereby giving Peroxide

Blonde a reason in her mind to justify her treatment of me. The pain and humiliation I felt as a result would both have been avoided if I'd worked out what my boundaries were in advance and stuck to them.

And sorry to sound unromantic about all this, but I believe that dating can often be a numbers game. No matter how confident you are, you may have to kiss a lot of frogs before you find your prince or princess.

The key is to have the confidence and self-belief to realize this. Some people settle for the frog, which is why they're unhappy. I'm now confident enough to carry on kissing because I know my princess is out there somewhere!

If you want to find out if Andy has finally met his princess, email him at andyj.mcgee@gmail.com.

in A Nutshell

∞ There will be times in life when you're faced with some choices that could ultimately affect your career, your earning potential and who you spend the rest of your life with.

∞ But these opportunities come with a price attached – it's going to cost you your place in your safe, secure and cosy comfort zone. You're going to have to step out into new territory and, what's more, you've got competition for the prize.

∞ Nerves are normal but you need to make sure you take steps to reduce your anxiety and avoid feeding your fears.

∞ Understand that your primitive brain's desire to protect you can sometimes undermine you.

Self-Confidence

No single idea or insight will cause you to shine out from the crowd. However, this chapter has given you over a dozen 10 percent tips and insights to help you turn the spotlight on your qualities and project yourself in the best possible light, whether that's speaking in public, being interviewed or going on a date.

Make sure you use them. And when you do, make sure you email me to let me know how they've helped you (sumo@paulmcgee.com).

8 What to Do When the Ship Hits the Flan

You're about to discover

Five
insights
and ideas to
help you recover
your confidence from
challenging setbacks.

Grieving is good.

It ain't what you see, it's the way
that you see it.

Park the pride.

Learn the lessons.

Molehills matter.

Setbacks Happen

In the chapter on "Who crushed your confidence?", we explored how people can crush, undermine and erode your confidence.

But it's not always about the impact of people.

Events, experiences and setbacks can all dramatically affect your self-belief and confidence. It could be a divorce, being made redundant, an illness, a car crash, the death of a loved one, a failed exam, a missed promotion or a period of unemployment.

And there's plenty more you could add to the list.

OK so there's the odd person who appears to coast through life, who seems almost immune from the challenges that beset the rest of us – at least on the surface, anyway.

But they're in the minority.

The rest of us are all likely at some stage to suffer a setback or challenge that rocks our steady world.

Pit Stop

- ∞ Review the list of events and setbacks mentioned above. Have you experienced any of these or something similar?
- ∞ Recall now how that experience affected you and your confidence.
- ∞ Look for ideas in this chapter that will help you if a similar event occurs in the future.
- ∞ Now think of someone you know who's having a tough time. Look for ideas to help rebuild their confidence.

The Personal Stuff

In this book you've read about me losing my job through ill health. Well here's how it all began.

April 1989, I think it was a Tuesday. I'd been summonsed to the company's head office, situated south west of London.

My wife Helen drove me there. She had to.
Having been diagnosed with ME (which is short for myalgic encephalomyelitis and is also known as chronic fatigue syndrome), I didn't have the energy to wash my own hair, so driving was clearly out of the question.

I was conscious that there was a certain amount of cynicism surrounding my illness. The press dubbed it "yuppie flu" and at times I seemed to be surrounded by well-meaning friends who had PhDs in coming up with crass comments.

"It's God's way of getting you to slow down," remarked one. Another approached me with his usual tact and diplomacy.

"You've got to be the luckiest bloke in the world, Paul. You sit around the house all day watching TV and doing absolutely nothing, while your wife works and then cooks your tea when she comes home. I envy you."

I sometimes imagine that if I'd had the energy I might have gently (well to begin with, anyway) squeezed his balls in a vice-like grip and used them to make earrings. While sarcastically adding.

"Thanks for your feedback, Dave. Your words of wisdom have really helped me come to terms with my debilitating illness that eight out of ten doctors are not even convinced is genuine. I feel a lot better now. Thank you."

But I didn't. After all, Dave was simply being Dave. What else did I expect?

Plus I was knackered. Completely knackered. I didn't have the energy to crush a grape, never mind Dave's testicles.

And so there I was. At head office. It seemed that all the people I spoke to that day were playing a game called "How to have a deep and meaningful conversation without ever making eye contact." They were ruddy good players.

Masterful, in fact.

Finally, after a series of management-speak meetings where lots was said but little actually understood, I was given the news.

"We're letting you go," said Kevin from Human Resources. He didn't even use my name.

"Letting me go. What do you mean?"

"Well, it's your illness. There's no way of telling when or even if you'll ever recover. We have no choice really."

"No choice," I muttered under my breath. You've plenty of bloody choices, I thought. In fact, let's get a flip-chart out and brainstorm what choices we do have.

"We will, of course, give you a month's notice," added Kevin generously.

"Er, thank you," I replied, as if I should be grateful for this immense act of kindness that was being bestowed on me from on high by the Human Resources department.

And that was it.

Five minutes later, with the aid of my walking stick and the guidance skills of Penny, Kevin's assistant, I found myself back in reception.

Helen, who'd been patiently waiting for me, looked up from the body-building magazines she'd been perusing. I told her the news. I no longer had a job.

The ship had well and truly hit the flan.

Whatever challenges you or those you know face, the key question is this:

How can you recover from such a setback?

And when your confidence is crumbling, how can you rebuild it?

Well, here's the good news.

You're about to discover how.

Your 10 Percent Tips on How to Rebuild and Recover Your Confidence

1 Grieving is good

Self-confidence is not another term for the art of self-delusion or self-deception. Appearing fine to the outside world when deep inside you're feeling pain and brokenness is not an effective approach. Self-confidence and vulnerability are not diametrically opposed – they're not like oil and water, they do mix.

The Personal Stuff

Our friend Chloe's marriage was a short one. In fact, very short. She got married just before Christmas and we enjoyed a meal with her and Graham, her new husband, at their home the following March. By May the relationship was over.

Chloe was devastated. For a while she became a virtual recluse. She carried on working, but rarely socialized with anybody. I guess she needed to grieve.

Her self-esteem seemed shattered but slowly, over time, the pieces were gradually put back together.

It did take time. It was a slow process.

And that's the key – it's a process.

There's no pill to pop that can eliminate the pain. There's no answer to give that can instantly heal the wounds.

You see, it's not time that's the healer.

It's the process.

And as Chloe worked through the loss of her dream, her marriage, she once again began to rebuild her confidence. But it still took time.

You can't rush grief.

We'd like to

but we can't.

It's a process – a journey that you go through. And pain, no matter how hard you try to avoid it, is part of the human experience.

Why we need to grieve

One of my principles is called "Hippo Time Is OK." Based on the fact that hippos wallow, it's a recognition that when a major setback occurs you cannot simply "get over it."

You do actually need a period of mourning, grieving and reflecting.

Often these emotions are associated with death, but they can relate to any form of loss you experience. Of course, the strength of those emotions and the length of time you experience them for will vary, depending on the event and its impact on you.

But you still need to take time to recover.

Sometimes your loss is very tangible, such as being made redundant or the breakdown of a relationship.

But grief can also relate to the loss or the ending of a hope or a dream – perhaps not getting the job you so desperately wanted or failing to buy the house you'd dreamt of owning.

These emotions are valid and not a sign of weakness. But to ignore or deny them can be emotionally damaging.

The truth is ...

Forget the stiff upper lip approach. Sometimes we need time to express, not suppress our pain.

However, let me make one thing clear:

This is not an invitation to pour your heart out in public and book yourself onto a daytime confessional television programme.

Grieving is good

but

it doesn't have to be high profile and it doesn't have to last too long.

Be careful when you're in this place.

Watch what you say to yourself during this time. If you're not careful, your own words will drag you further and deeper into the mud.

A useful statement to make to yourself during your grieving or wallowing would be:

I'm OK, and I'm not OK. I'm still the person I was before this event, with all my strengths and qualities. But I'm also hurting from what's happened. However, these feelings are temporary and they do not define me. Neither will this event determine my future – my response to what's happened will be the determining factor.

I allow myself to feel low, to feel angry and to feel pain. That is a healthy and normal response. But I will not remain feeling low, angry and in pain. This is temporary. It's part of my journey. It's not my destination.

I will pull through – if I choose to. And that's what I choose to do.

Because deep down, at the centre of who I am, I know I'm still OK.

(If you would like to download the above, please visit www. TheSumoGuy.com.)

The truth is ...

Grieving is good - for a time. To wallow is not a weakness - neither is it a way of life.

Pit Stop

∞ What are your feelings about what you've just read? Do you grieve too much or not enough?
∞ When did you last grieve over a loss?
∞ How long did your grieving last?
∞ How do you get yourself going again?

The Personal Stuff

Becoming ill with ME (or chronic fatigue syndrome) has to have been one of the biggest challenges of my life.

After my diagnosis I worked hard at remaining optimistic and convinced myself that full recovery was around the corner. I was known as a positive person and I wanted to live up to my reputation. If I told people how I genuinely felt and was honest about my fears, I believed that would be a sign of weakness.

You see, if I was being totally honest I knew that my illness was not life-threatening, but it could be life-limiting. And questions danced around my mind.

Would I ever work again?

Would we have kids?

Would I end up in a wheelchair?

It took me some time to wake up to the fact that it was OK to grieve not just for the loss of my health, but for the loss of my job and the loss of the future I'd hoped for.

I didn't share my grief with everyone, but Helen, my wife, was and remains my confidant. She'd previously listened to my dreams. Now she listened to my despair. She knew my aspirations but now she knew my anguish.

It's not easy to grieve alone – we need other people to share our burden. Fortunately, I found my burden carrier in my wife and a few close friends.

I hope that when you need to grieve you also find the same level of support.

But a word of warning. Whatever you do, make sure that your supporters are not Awfulisers (see Chapter 3) – you've got enough problems as it is without their help.

That's the first insight on how to rebuild and recover your confidence when the ship hits the flan. Let's look at another really important idea.

2   It ain't what you see, it's the way that you see it

Here's something I find interesting. Have you ever noticed that two people can experience the same event, the same setback, and yet react completely differently? For one person the setback could be the final straw, while the other simply laughs it off.

The truth is ...

> A stumbling block to one person is a stepping stone for someone else.

So how can you be the person who uses a setback as a stepping stone? How can you respond more effectively when the ship hits the flan?

The key is perspective.

How you see the event, and the *meaning* you attach to it, will determine how you respond.

Sounds simple, doesn't it?

It's not.

It requires a rational approach – and, as you've discovered already, that's not easy. The reality is that as humans we're far more emotional creatures than we are rational. When trouble strikes we are rarely rational.

And that's understandable. Emotions are what make us human. But we often allow them to derail us and distort our picture of reality. Emotions affect how we see the world.

Why do two people respond differently to the same event? Because we don't see the world for what it is. We see the world *as we are*.

And if you're *feeling* very differently from someone else then you're also *seeing* very differently as well.

The truth is ...

Your perception
of a situation is
not the reality.

Let me explain.

If I'm feeling victimized, unloved and lacking in hope, it's highly unlikely that I'll be seeing the world as a great place. Equally, if I'm feeling empowered, loved and positive about my future, the world takes on a new perspective.

The world hasn't changed.

My perspective has.

And my perspective has been influenced by how I'm feeling at that time.

Which is OK, as long as I then don't allow my emotions to hijack my rational perspective and hold me hostage indefinitely.

You see, there's something extremely powerful and important to remember.

The truth is ...

Feelings are not facts.

Those four words could be worth far more than a 10 percent change to you. This insight is profound.

It's powerful.

Make sure that you repeat it to yourself regularly, particularly when emotionally you feel that the world is going to end or you can see no possible way out of your situation.

Let me expand further. To feel a particular emotion such as anger, fear or rejection is natural and normal. The key is to remember that these emotions don't by themselves define you or your situation.

And despite what some authors argue, it's not easy to change your emotions in an instant. We're complex beings.

It's not as simple as deciding to click your fingers or switch a button and see your emotions change.

So what can you do?

You can decide while still experiencing your emotions to detach yourself from their power and control over you. I explored some strategies on how to do this in the previous chapter. Here are some more.

Use the following phrases to help you:

∞ "I'm aware that at the moment I'm experiencing feelings of ..." (You're identifying the emotion and in doing so, you're owning it, rather than it owning you.)
∞ "I acknowledge why I'm feeling this way (mentally go through the list of reasons as you see them), but I'm aware that my feeling are not facts."
∞ "I'm conscious that my feelings fluctuate, and will distort my perspective – so now is not the time to make an important decision."
∞ "Although I feel ... I could do ... to help myself." (You can fill in the blanks.)

To assist you in seeing things differently and gain a clearer perspective on your situation, the following two questions will also help:

∞ "Where is this issue on a scale of 1–10 (where 10 = death)?"
∞ "How important will this be in six months' time?"

Remember, the goal is not to eradicate your emotions – that is dangerous and ultimately unachievable. But your ability to recover your self-esteem and confidence after a setback will be affected by your relationship with your emotions and the power you give to them.

And there's more ...

Your perspective on your problem will also be influenced by the following insights I gained from reading the work of Anthony Robbins. They are worth reflecting on and remembering.

∞ *Problems are not personal.* They are not conspiring to get at you personally. It might sometimes feel that way, but it's not. Problems happen to all of us.

∞ *Problems are not pervasive.* Just because you have experienced a setback or disappointment in one area of your life doesn't mean that it will automatically occur in other areas as well. Life does have ups and downs. But remember, in the board game of life there are ladders as well as snakes. The only thing is, when you're feeling down you can fail to notice the ladders. You ignore the positives and believe that everything is going against you. The reality is that it's not. But beware. Problems can and do spread if you resign yourself to the fact they will.

∞ *Problems are not permanent.* They might seem that way at the moment, but things can and do change. How soon they change will depend on you and your response. But if you're locked into the disempowering belief that "there's nothing I can do," then clearly things will take longer to improve. However, if you ask the question "How can I influence or improve the situation?" then your perspective of the problem changes. At the heart of that question lies an empowering belief that things can change.

No matter how bad the situation looks at the moment, remember, the truth is ...

> # Everything
> # is
> # temporary.

∞ How would you rate your current challenges on a scale of 1–10 (where 10 = death)?

∞ How important will these issues be in six months' time?

∞ Identify one key challenge you have at the moment. How could you influence or improve the situation? What's the first thing you need to do?

∞ Which insight about your problem was particularly helpful?

Problems are not personal.

Problems are not pervasive.

Problems are not permanent.

So far I've explored how when the ship hits the flan you can maintain or recover your self-confidence by remembering:

∞ Grieving is good.
∞ It ain't what you see, it's the way that you see it.

Now let's explore the third strategy to help you recover from a setback.

3 Park the pride

Although your setback or challenge may be humbling, that's not to say you'll be humble enough to ask for help. Your sense of pride may prevent you from doing so.

Bad move.

Believing that you can recover from your setback completely unaided is noble, but also nonsense.

There's a phrase that says, "If it's got to be, it's up to me." I agree. But I don't interpret that as "it's up to me *alone.*"

You will need to take action.

You will need the inner drive and determination to recover, but it's not necessary to do this without the help of others.

The truth is ...

> To call upon the support and strength of others is not an indication of weakness - it's a sign of wisdom.

The Personal Stuff

My friend Steve's divorce was a messy one. Actually, he would describe the breakdown of his marriage as traumatic. It wasn't the arguments about who got the plasma TV or the cat, but the psychological damage that affected him most.

If words have the power of life and death, then Steve felt his ex-wife was a master at dealing out the death cards. It's what had undermined their marriage, and now it was undermining his confidence.

But Steve was brave. Too brave.

"I was respected in my profession, I mentored several guys. People came to me for advice; I was the one who was seen to have all the answers," he says. "So I kept my despair to myself."

"Professionally I remained competent and in control – but personally I felt close to a breakdown. My world was shattered, but I didn't want any help in picking up the pieces."

It was over a year before Steve asked for help, and even longer before he began gradually to see the restoring and rebuilding of his self-esteem and confidence.

"Pride was my biggest problem. I felt asking for help was a sign of weakness. I don't know about whether it's better to give than to receive, but from my experience it's a damn sight easier."

Fortunately Steve's mates were able to help him, but that was only after he parked his pride and admitted he needed some help.

Parking the pride means drawing on the support of others, something we looked at extensively in the chapter "You'll get by with a little help from your friends." The role of the Confidant could be particularly helpful when you've suffered a setback, and make sure you spend time with your Cheerleaders (see Chapter 5).

Pit Stop

- ∞ How much could you relate to how Steve dealt with his problem?
- ∞ In what ways has that approach helped or hindered you?
- ∞ How easy do you find asking others for help?
- ∞ Who in your world might need your help at the moment?

4 Learn the lessons

It's OK to make mistakes – as long as you don't repeat them. That's good advice.

But as you know already, applying it is not so easy.

Redundancy, divorce or a failed promotion can destabilize you. However, the experience is not just one to recover from, but also one to learn from.

When you fail to look for the lessons from your experience it's hard to find any positives.

And you're more likely to repeat the same mistakes.

It's an easy and common trap to fall into (that's why people keep falling into debt – they don't learn from their mistakes).

Life as you see it may have dealt you a blow.

But it may also have taught you an invaluable lesson.

If you're prepared to look for it.

To help you learn the lessons, here are some great questions to reflect on when you've had a setback in life:

∞ What has this experience taught me about myself?
∞ What has it taught me about other people?
∞ What have I learnt about life from this experience?
∞ If I were to face a similar event or experience in the future, what would I do differently?
∞ If I had to give a talk to a group of students about my experience, what would be my top three pieces of advice?

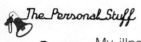

My illness taught me a lot about life, myself and other people. For at least a couple of years I saw it as an episode that would remain firmly locked away in the filing cabinet of life's experiences. It might sound melodramatic, but the whole experience would have been filed away under the letter "d" for devastating. I wasn't keen to reopen it.

However, when I finally felt able to reflect on the episode in more detail, the folder contained more than I'd expected.

I learnt that some people are amazing. My wife headed that particular list.

I learnt that some people with great intentions can have an appalling impact. And be completely blind to the fact.

I learnt that illness doesn't discriminate and whatever I say, do, believe or think, I'm not immune from it.

I learnt that small victories are important. I celebrated when I was able to walk 20 metres without my walking stick, and when I went a whole day without needing a sleep.

I learnt that I'm incredibly impatient. I wanted my recovery to be rapid. I wanted to fast forward through the experience, when actually I needed to press pause.

I learnt that recovery is often gradual and takes time.

I learnt that setbacks are often part of the recovery process.

I learnt that it's OK to have crap days and admit to having them.

I learnt that it's important never to give up and to do all you can to look for the positive.

I learnt that illness is as much of a psychological battle as it is a physical one.

I learnt that I'm more resilient than I realized.

I learnt that my recovery may help other people's recovery.

I guess you could say I learnt a lot – but only when I was prepared and ready to learn the lessons.

Pit Stop

∞ What are you learning from your experience? (Remember life may have dealt you a blow, but it's also taught you an invaluable lesson.) Review the list of questions on page [216] and answer them now.

∞ Which of those questions is most helpful for you and why?

Here's my fifth and final insight on how to recover your confidence when the ship hits the flan.

5   Molehills matter

When my football team loses, the manager often replies that it's important they bounce back. It's a phrase he uses a lot. Sadly.

The term "bounce back" has a sense of immediacy and urgency about it. When you've had a minor setback it's a helpful goal to have. Asking yourself "What are the three actions I need to take now in order to bounce back?" is a great question.

However, sometimes an event or experience has such a deep impact on you that the phrase "bouncing back" hardly seems appropriate.

You don't bounce back from a bereavement or a divorce. It's not that easy. The recovery time is longer. Having said that, neither do you want to remain permanently down after a particularly challenging, damaging or difficult experience. Grieving is good – but not indefinitely.

So how do you recover? How do you climb the mountain?

You start with molehills.

Forget the mountain. It's too large and probably looks too difficult to climb.

But molehills?

They're small.

They're achievable.

Climb enough molehills and over time you're confident enough to try hill climbing. And when you've had the momentum to climb hills, you've got the belief and inspiration to climb mountains.

But you start with the molehill.

The truth is ...

Never discount the importance and significance of a small step in the right direction.

No matter how small they are, actions add up. A 10 percent change makes a difference. That's the whole premise of this book.

Remember, slowly and sometimes subtly your confidence is growing through the actions you're taking.

Maybe it's just having the courage to leave your house, or to smile at a stranger. Maybe it's returning to work – even though it's only part time.

Maybe it's saying "yes" to just one invitation.

It doesn't matter how small. It's a start.

It's creating momentum. The progress may be small, but it's still progress. It's still worth acknowledging and celebrating. It might only be a small victory – but it's still a victory.

And with victory comes hope.

The Personal Stuff

One day I put on my suit. It still fitted me – just. I had spent over two years wearing jeans. There's no need to dress up when you're going to the post office to collect your invalidity benefit. There's no dress code.

But I felt well enough this particular day to drive into town. I perhaps couldn't walk too far, but I wouldn't need my walking stick.

Wearing my suit that day made me feel good. It made me feel normal.

People looking at me would presume I was an office worker on his lunch. They would see my suit.

I didn't wear my suit again for over six months. But it was a start. It gave me a taste of what being well would actually look and feel like in reality. It felt good.

I guess some people could mock such a minor achievement. But it would only be minor to them.

To me it was another step towards my recovery. To me it was another victory. It was a molehill, but it mattered.

Pit Stop

∞ What's the one simple action, no matter how small, you could take this week to boost your confidence?

∞ Why take that particular action? What will be the benefit?

∞ Now imagine how you'd feel once you've done it.

Why don't you email me once you've taken the action, sumo@paulmcgee.com, and let me know how it helped? I promise I'll read your email.

in A Nutshell

When the ship hits the flan your self-confidence can crumble under the weight of the experience. The damage at first may seem irreparable. But they only write off cars – they don't write off people. Recovery may take time, but it is achievable. The following will definitely help the process:

∞ Grieving is good – for a time.
∞ It ain't what you see, it's the way that you see it. Avoid allowing your emotions to hijack and distort the reality of your situation.
∞ Park the pride – recovery is not a road to travel alone.
∞ Learn the lessons – life is your greatest teacher, but learning is still optional.
∞ Molehills matter – small victories add up.

9 How to Handle Conflict Confidently

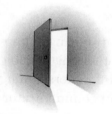

You're about to discover

The consequences
of conflict handled
badly.

Ten things that make
people aggressive.

Four insights regarding conflict
to be aware of.

Four strategies to enhance
your communication.

Let's be honest, communication between people can be a minefield. Emotions, egos and differing personalities can create an explosive cocktail. Yet communication is at the heart of all we do whether at home or work. And the quality of our communication can have a profound impact on the quality of our relationships and ultimately the quality of our lives.

Step into the minefield of communication with a shoulder bag of self-doubt and poor self-esteem and the chances of making it safely to the other side are slim. As a result too many people carry the scars of conflict.

And yet it doesn't have to be that way. Learning to communicate more clearly and confidently is not an unattainable skill. With the right insight, awareness and understanding you can learn to become a more confident communicator. You can learn the skills to avoid conflict situations, and when they are unavoidable, to diffuse them rather than see them escalate. Like learning to ride a bike, personality and background do not determine your effectiveness but skill and practise do. And that's what this chapter is about. Learning to communicate more effectively in conflict situations.

The Consequences of Conflict Handled Badly

It's strange isn't it? We can learn all about the conflicts of the past between countries, we can learn about the conflicts of the present between celebrities and yet rarely do we learn how to deal with our own personal conflicts. I might have learnt about the Battle of Hastings in 1066 and the history of two world wars at school but I didn't learn the necessary skills on how to handle conflict in my own life.

Sadly some people's only conflict training manual comes from the latest soap opera or reality TV show. Verbal aggression, which at times can lead to violence, is seen by some as an inevitable destination when two people fail to see eye to eye. Meanwhile others take the road of passive acceptance or avoidance as their approach to dealing with conflict.

Unfortunately the latter approach can encourage bullying, being taken for granted and a complete lack of respect for who we are.

Given such potential outcomes some may be surprised that "the art of getting on with others" is not seen as a compulsory subject on the school curriculum.

So what about you? When it comes to conflict are you more inclined to be an Avoider, an Aggressor or an Assertive?

Perhaps you'll relate to all three approaches.

Depending on the situation and context you may slip in and out of each response.

The Way of the Avoider

When an issue is not that important you may choose to be an Avoider. You make a conscious decision to avoid conflict because the outcome is not that important to you. Perhaps the prize of a peaceful life is greater than the need to achieve another outcome. Avoidance is a strategy you can use that helps you avoid conflict in the first place.

The truth is...

You don't have to feel compelled to assert yourself in every situation.

Using the avoidance strategy may be a conscious decision on your part. For instance, when it comes to your relationship with your children you may decide to lose a particular battle in order to win the war. You may take the same approach with a customer, colleague or friend. In other words you decide to back down on what you consider to be a minor issue in order to help you achieve the outcome you want on a bigger, more important issue.

And that's fine.

When the strategy works.

When the strategy is a conscious choice on your part.

But what about when it's your only strategy?

What about when it's your natural default approach?

What about when it's more to do with your unconscious behaviour than a conscious decision?

The consequences of being an Avoider

Using this as your one and only approach to conflict situations can result in the following:

∞ It's seen as a sign of weakness
∞ You're perceived as a soft touch
∞ Your credibility can plummet
∞ People lose respect for you
∞ You can lose respect for yourself
∞ Your avoidance is seen as acceptance
∞ Your avoidance can encourage others to continue to behave the way they are
∞ You can inwardly develop anger and resentment

They're not great outcomes are they?

But they will be your outcomes if you go through life using avoidance as your only strategy to conflict situations.

And the reason for this approach?

In a nutshell you lack the self-confidence and know-how to deal with things differently.

So avoidance is one way of dealing with conflict. Now let's explore another.

The Way of the Aggressor

For an Aggressor there is only one way to deal with conflict and that is through attack. Diplomacy is dated. Understanding another person's perspective is not an option. A flexible approach is something only relevant to gymnasts.

And yet although people act aggressively their reasons for doing so may vary.

Can you identify with any of the following?

∞ Perhaps you know you can get away with being aggressive
∞ You believe it's the only way to achieve the result you want
∞ You've learnt this approach from the role models around you
∞ You believe it's expected of you and constitutes normal behaviour (this being especially the case with men)
∞ You believe any other approach would be seen as a sign of weakness
∞ You lack regard or consideration for the other person's perspective
∞ You lack the necessary skills or understanding to change your aggressive behaviour into assertive behaviour
∞ Your view of the world is black and white. There are winners and losers. End of story. You fail to appreciate the concept of win/win
∞ You're stressed and your aggression is a symptom of an underlying problem
∞ You've reached stalemate with the other person and what you consider to be their inflexible approach causes you frustration which in turn builds into aggression

The consequences of being an Aggressor

Just as the reasons for an aggressive approach can vary, so can the consequences. Relationships can be damaged, people can feel victimized, fire can be met with fire. And yet, despite these potentially negative outcomes, an aggressive response can lead in some cases to the outcome you want. It can shake the other person or party from their complacency, it can bring things to a head, it can be your way of standing up to the aggression of others.

I would not advocate this as a great strategy to use in life as the risks of such behaviour are invariably damaging. But I am not naive enough to ignore the fact that there are rare occasions when such an approach may bring about the outcome you want. It is perhaps a last resort for some people – but for others it's the only approach they know.

Pit Stop

- ∞ What tends to be your most common approach to dealing with conflict: aggression or avoidance?
- ∞ When you are aggressive which one of the previous factors is the cause of it?
- ∞ Reflect on some of the conflict situations you have encountered. What has been the consequence of your approach?
- ∞ How happy have you been with those consequences?

How to Become More Confident and Assertive in Conflict Situations

Most people I come across don't enjoy or welcome conflict. There has been the occasional exception, particularly the manager I met who said she enjoyed disciplining people as part of her role.

She was an interesting woman.

But there aren't many who welcome conflict. Perhaps those people who do seem to enjoy it – or are certainly not fazed by it – have both the confidence *and* the competence to handle it effectively.

But whether or not we enjoy it, the reality is it's difficult to avoid. And unless you're a Trappist monk living in some remote monastery who has undertaken a vow of silence, it's perhaps an inevitable part of life.

So how do we get better at it?

Here are four great insights to be aware of:

1 Recognize it's OK

Conflicts, disagreements and misunderstandings are not wrong. They are an inevitable consequence of living in a fast-paced, ever-changing and ever-expanding world. Just recognize that fact.

In fact, life without conflict is both boring and bland. Disagreement can be the crucible out of which creative and new ideas are born.

So don't buy into the lie that conflict is wrong. It's not the conflict itself that is wrong – but when it is handled badly things invariably do go wrong. The downfall of the former British Prime Minister Margaret Thatcher illustrates this brilliantly. The conflict arose due to disagreement amongst her cabinet over the Poll Tax, but the poor way it was handled led to her departure. History is littered with such examples from every walk of life, and from both ends of the political spectrum.

The truth is...

> Conflict is inevitable. However, fighting is optional.

2 Recognize reality rules

Where there are people there are problems. Sorry to sound negative, but it's true.

People are different.

Difficult. Complex. Stubborn. Carry baggage.

Have different agendas. Priorities. Beliefs. Upbringings.

Have unrealistic expectations. Different tolerances to stress. Health issues. Self-awareness issues.

The truth is...

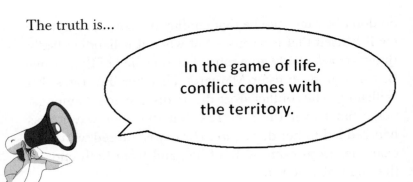

In the game of life, conflict comes with the territory.

3 Recognize your rights

Ever heard someone say "I know my rights" when making a complaint? The fact is we rarely think about what rights we should expect to have as a citizen on this planet. So how about chewing over the following:

You have the right... to deal with others without being dependent on them for approval.

You don't have to have everyone telling you you're an OK worthwhile person to be an OK worthwhile person. Quit having the goal that life is about getting everybody to like and accept you. That belief is born out of insecurity, not self-confidence. Of course we want people to like us but look for ideas in this book to learn how to like and accept yourself which is not based entirely on other people's opinion of you. And drop the notion that it's possible to please everyone all of the time.

It isn't.

So get used to it.

The truth is...

Insecurity fuels the desire to persistently want to please people.

When that is your goal you will do all you can to avoid conflict or disagreement with others. Wanting to please other people is fine but if it's done only in order to achieve acceptance and approval then you have a problem.

You have the right... to have your ideas and opinions listened to and accepted as valid and important for you.

People might not agree with your opinions and sometimes your ideas might not always be well thought through – but you still have the right to express them.

You have the right... to say "no" to requests without feeling guilty or selfish.

Clearly using this approach consistently will not win you many friends and you may be viewed as unhelpful. But you do have the right to say "no", OK? Remember you cannot permanently please people all of the time.

e.g. "I appreciate your invitation but I'm going to have to decline. Thank you."

You have the right... to set clear boundaries.

Please don't fall into the trap of expecting people to be mind readers and then resent them for when they're not. Clearly set out what you can and cannot do for someone.

e.g. "Yes I will be happy to work through my lunch hour but I will need to leave promptly at 5pm."

You have the right... to ask for time to think things over.

Don't always give in to the demands people make to give them an instant answer. When appropriate take your time.

e.g. "I recognize you're after a quick decision but I will need some time to carefully consider this. I will get back to you with an answer tomorrow morning. OK?"

You have the right... to decline feeling responsible for other people's problems.

Be careful to avoid being taken on a guilt trip. If you're not careful people will be dumping their problems on you. You may choose to help someone but this does not mean you automatically have to just because you have been asked to.

e.g. "I appreciate you have some financial problems and want me to help. However, I think you're going to have to look for other ways in which you can reduce your debt."

And if you're happy to help someone remember to set clear boundaries.

e.g. "Yes I'm happy to meet up with you. Come to my house for 7:30pm but remember I need to be free by 9:30pm to put the kids to bed."

You have the right... to be treated with respect.

Whatever your job title, status or background you are a human being and are entitled to be treated so.

Pit Stop

∞ Which of the above "rights" do you need to consciously focus on?
∞ Which if any do you think are unrealistic?
∞ Choose one of the above and type it up as a reminder for yourself.

Recognising you have rights is only one side of the bargain, however. If we are to communicate confidently in conflict situations we also need to be aware of our responsibilities.

4   Recognize your responsibilities

You have the responsibility... to accept that other people have their own opinions, feelings, views and ideas, which may be different from your own.

And these may never change. Sometimes you have to accept you will need to agree to disagree. And that's OK.

You have the responsibility... to talk in a clear way to others so they understand your needs.

Perhaps the breakdown in communication is not down to the other person but due to us being vague and unclear in how we have put across our views.

You have the responsibility... to accept the consequences of your actions and decisions, particularly when you choose not to assert yourself.

It can be easy to see ourselves as put upon and to play the role of victim. Accept that this may be the price you pay for a passive response. It didn't automatically happen – your response contributed to the outcome.

You have the responsibility... to recognize that other people may choose not to be involved in resolving your problems.

Clearly communicate your needs and express your expectations of others but recognize that people will have their own reasons, some justified and some perhaps not, for not getting involved. Remember they also have rights.

You have the responsibility... to ensure you do not make unreasonable demands of others in order to alleviate your own stress.

That's an important point to be aware of. Is there someone close to you who you are placing unreasonable demands on?

Pit Stop

- ∞ Take some time to review the list of responsibilities. If you had to choose two to be more conscious of in the next seven days which would you choose?
- ∞ Reflect on a situation in your personal or professional life where your awareness of these two "*responsibilities*" will lead to you dealing with a situation differently.
- ∞ Will this insight result in you actually avoiding a potential conflict situation or see you managing one more effectively?

How to Have an Uncomfortable Conversation

Here are four strategies to deal with a potentially tricky conflict situation with greater confidence.

Be prepared

I first learnt that as a motto when I was a boy scout. There's heaps of wisdom contained within those two words and their advice is particularly important when you're about to have an uncomfortable conversation. Perhaps the most important question is not

"Do I feel confident?"

But

"Am I confident I have all the facts?"

Progressing the conversation without having all the facts is like running the 100 metres on quick sand – you won't get very far. Your aim is to get as many of the facts beforehand as you can. Confidence rises as preparation increases. This conversation is unlikely to be easy or straightforward but if you embark upon it without any real preparation you'll soon find yourself quickly sinking. Don't allow any misguided confidence to get in the way of adequate preparation. Without it your confidence will last about as long as an overinflated balloon in a needle factory.

The truth is

Confidence comes from clarity.

Focus on feelings and facts

Remember your goal is not to gain a victory or win a battle but to resolve a conflict. In order to do so you need a strategy. A list of random ill-thought-through accusations will do little for your credibility or confidence. But being clear on where you're going and the journey required to get there will. Here's a very simple and yet very effective approach:

State the facts and then elaborate on how those facts make you feel.

For example:

> *"I didn't appreciate how you spoke to me during the team meeting on Tuesday. Suggesting that my comments on how to improve customer service were 'naff' was not helpful at all (**The facts**). I felt undermined in front of my colleagues and now feel a lot less confident about putting forward other ideas in the future (**The feelings**)."*

Or if it's related to home life:

> *"I'm conscious that when I talk to you about whether you've done your homework you usually reply that 'I'm getting heavy with you and I don't trust you' (**The facts**). I only want the best for you but feel that I can't ask you about your homework anymore without feeling that I'm nagging you (**The feelings**)."*

Your goal at this stage is not to deliver a knockout blow and to make the other person look stupid. It is very simply to express the facts as you interpret them and then to calmly communicate how you feel as a result.

Save their face

No one enjoys being criticized or challenged and although that is not necessarily your intention, uncomfortable conversations can create defensiveness in people. And when someone feels defensive one course of action is to strike out.

So how can you decrease this potential response?

Do what you can to help the other person save face.

For instance you might say

"I appreciate when you made that comment it wasn't your intention to..."

Or

"Look, it was a simple mistake that we've all made. I'm probably the biggest culprit. However..."

Now be careful you don't go overboard with this approach. You still need to be clear on the facts and your feelings, but also take into account their feelings. When you do so you make moving onto the next step far easier.

Be solution focused

Your goal in resolving conflict is not to make the other person squirm and to heap guilt and condemnation on them. Although I appreciate that last sentence has now caused you to let out a long sigh of disappointment. But it isn't is it?

OK, I confess that the thought of seeing some people squirm and squeal in the face of your comments may actually be quite appealing, but that's not supposed to be our goal!

Our goal is to see a solution – not carry out a crucifixion.

Agree?

So what's the best way to achieve that?

Well some questions you might want to ask are:

"How can we best resolve this?"

Or

"How can we prevent that happening again?"

By asking questions you're including the other person in the solution. This in itself is a great way to help them avoid losing face. It's also moving the conversation from what might, however unintentionally, be seen as the territory of "blame and shame" to "back in the game". It's helping move the conflict on to resolution.

And people are more likely to buy into a solution that they've been part of.

However, that is only one approach.

You may decide, depending on the context, that the approach you wish to take is simply to state your solution or desire for the future.

For example:

"I would really appreciate it if, in the future..."

Or

"This is how I would like the matter resolved..."

It's important you have a good idea of how you want the conflict resolved. It might not be the perfect outcome but you need to be clear on what you will accept as a better outcome. And remember:

The truth is...

You're not here to fix the blame; you're here to fix the problem.

- ∞ Review the four approaches "Be prepared", "Focus on feelings and facts", "Save their face" and "Be solution focused". Which one in particular do you need to be more conscious of using in the future?
- ∞ What benefits will using this approach bring to you and the other person?
- ∞ Who else could you involve to help resolve an issue you're facing?
- ∞ Which approach would you say you are already using to good effect?

The Personal Stuff

I write this chapter very much based on personal experience. My roles as manager, father, husband and now managing director of my own company have at times provided me with the occasional need for an uncomfortable conversation. And I would love to say I always follow my own advice – but I haven't – particularly when it comes to my family. I have said and done things I have regretted. But I have chosen to go easy on the boxing gloves (See Chapter 6 "How to be your own best mate"). And as a result I have learnt from, rather than been condemned by, my mistakes.

My biggest single lesson has been: "Don't strike whilst the iron is hot".

When you do, people get burnt.

I have also learnt that proving the other person wrong is not the goal – resolving a misunderstanding or a problem is.

There are times in my relationship with my wife Helen where we have "agreed to disagree" and I'm conscious that when emotions run high, rational thinking often runs low.

Recently what had the potential to be an exciting conversation became an uncomfortable one. A general lack of space at home, coupled with our deserved "Most cluttered house in Britain" award meant I felt we were in desperate need to move house.

Helen saw things differently. Whilst recognising the problem, she saw a different solution. Extend. Build onto the side of the house – problem solved and at a much cheaper price than moving.

She had a point.

The cost of paying stamp duty to the government just for the pleasure of moving alone would make a substantial dent in what was required to pay for an extension.

Rationally speaking we should stay. Problem was I had seen the details of a house which I immediately fell in love with. Helen, however, was prepared to start examining the facts and explore potential solutions. So we put our house up for sale in a low key way. In other words, we didn't put up a "For Sale" board and chose the highest value of those presented by the estate agents. We were laying a bait and seeing if we got a bite.

Then as a family we visited the house that had caught my attention.

I was sold.

So were the kids.

Helen liked it but had several reservations. And she was not planning on playing the role of the Avoider.

Conflict began to brew.

My temptation was to be the Aggressor; to steamroller through my ideas and persuade Helen through emotion and the strength of my desire.

I gave into my temptation.

Such an approach immediately created tension. When a cavalier approach meets a cautious one, conflict is inevitable.

Two things needed to happen.

I needed to take my foot off the enthusiasm pedal and Helen needed to be heard.

Clearly we were not going to move if one of us was very opposed to the idea.

But Helen felt under pressure. Pressure not just from me but from the kids as well. My teenage daughter Ruth would finally have a place big enough for her handbags, shoes and makeup. My son would have room to entertain his mates in an area somewhat bigger than his existing postage-stamp-sized bedroom.

And what I thought would be the clincher – Helen would have more space in which to accumulate clutter and the 147 photo albums that we never look at.

But Helen was unconvinced. It may have been five against one (sorry, I forgot to mention, the cats were up for moving as well), but without Helen's buy-in we were staying.

So what did I do?

I decided to Shut Up

and

Listen.

Helen felt defensive.

And rightly so – she was being totally irrational.

Just kidding.

But when you're feeling defensive and under pressure it's hard to be rational in your thinking. And we were destined for an emotional argument, not a logical discussion.

So I applied the brakes to my own ideas and started listening to her concerns. The goal was not to get her to see things my way but for me to understand her way.

We focused on the facts and how Helen was feeling.

By listening and talking things through we got to what was at the heart of her concerns.

I found agreement in much of what she said.

Helen also listened to me and my thoughts.

We looked at our finances rather than speculate about our feelings.

We got advice from our financial adviser.

I got used to the idea of staying.

It was good to talk, but more importantly it was good to listen. To each other.

We went to see the house a second time.

Helen still had her doubts about moving. And I understood those causes for concern.

But I did feel confident.

Not that we would move house, but that whatever conclusion we arrived at we had done so by applying a little more light and a little less heat to our conversation.

So what was the outcome? Did we move?

Well we have just accepted an offer on our house.

And we have had an offer accepted on the house that we all became keen on.

It might all still fall through. Some things are outside our control.

But whatever the outcome I think we've all learnt lessons about ourselves and also how to deal with others in potentially difficult and emotional situations.

in A Nutshell

∞ Conflict is an inevitable part of life. A lack of confidence and competence in handling it can create further problems and potentially lead to damaged relationships.

∞ It's important to realize there is not "a right way" to deal with conflict but there are some effective ways to ensure you are more likely to increase your chances of dealing with it successfully.

∞ It's worth remembering that as human beings we do have some basic rights and responsibilities. Being aware of both will help us deal more confidently with conflict situations and perhaps even prevent them from occurring.

∞ Our goal ultimately is to resolve issues and find solutions when possible. Life and relationships are rarely straightforward – in fact they are sometimes messy. But using the ideas and insights in this chapter will result in better if not perfect outcomes.

10 Have You Got the Confidence to Go M.A.D.?

You're about to discover

The importance
of using your
increased confidence
to benefit others, not
just yourself.

The payoffs you receive when you
seek to help others.

How to move out of your comfort zone to
make a difference.

We've been on quite a journey. We've explored both how and why confidence can be the catalyst to your success. It's clearly not the only factor that can help you achieve your potential, but it's a hugely important one.

Take self-confidence out of the equation and it affects where you go and what you do. And as we've discovered, a little change in your level of confidence can, over time, make a big difference.

We've also sought to take the "con" out of confidence. There is no magic pill that propels us to a different level. Dancing naked is not the answer (particularly when driving) and self-doubt can never be totally banished. But neither should it master us.

We've learnt that confidence is situational – people are not confident in *everything* they do, unless they're desperately deluded or overwhelmed by their own arrogance. And alcohol may seem like a short-term quick fix, but it's definitely not a long-term cure.

We then went on to play the "explain game" as we examined who crushed your confidence. Our past can haunt us. But confronting and exploring the issues of our personal history can help us to understand our present and then release us to move on more confidently into the future.

As we've seen, people make mistakes – rarely deliberately, often unintentionally. But their words and actions can either infuse us with confidence or gradually erode it.

However, perhaps the biggest culprit in undermining your confidence is looking back at you in the mirror.

You can be your own worst enemy.

The point to remember is that by understanding the causes of our problems, we're better placed to deal with them.

The focus of our journey then changed. The scenery became different as we looked at how to build, or in some cases rebuild, our confidence. The route to recovery requires the support of others. To enjoy emotionally healthy balanced lives, we need people who are our Cheerleaders, Challengers, Coaches and Confidants.

As the terrain changes, so do our requirements as to which type of person or role would be most helpful. Flipflops are great for sandy beaches but less so when climbing a mountain. Equally, Cheerleaders can be fantastic encouragers, but if you're basking in a sea of complacency then you'll find they're not what you require.

We then took time to explore perhaps the single most important relationship in your life: the one with yourself. At times you can be your own worst critic. In many ways this is normal, but over time it can be damaging if you don't take the necessary precautions.

So accept that flaws are us, go easy on the boxing glove and do a spot of DIY plastic surgery on your mind. If such a metaphor seems too extreme, then see working on your mindset as taking medicine for the mind. The important point to remember is that the conversations we have with ourselves are crucial. So take control of the content.

We've looked at specific situations when you want to shine if your neck's on the line. It's important to understand that increased confidence does not eradicate anxiety or pressure. Neither does it eliminate our feeling of discomfort. The skill comes when we face our challenges and seize our opportunities in spite of how we're feeling.

We learnt a very important lesson – feelings are not facts. And by being better prepared and developing our abilities, confidence can begin to take root and flourish. We've also learnt techniques on how to minimize and master the negative impact of our emotions.

Finally, we explored how even increased confidence still doesn't make you immune from life's challenges. Redundancy, illness, bereavement and divorce can all appear on the horizon and if you don't know how to navigate, the ship can literally hit the flan.

Therefore it's important to recognize that grieving is good – for a time. We need to wallow. But it's not appropriate to stay there. It's part of our journey – it's not our destination.

We also need to recognize that it ain't what you see, it's the way that you see it, and to look for the lessons from our experiences. Collisions do occur, but we can limit the damage – our life doesn't have to be a write-off. And make sure that you create some momentum by climbing some molehills.

OK. So far so good?

Great.

Now what?

As a result of our journey so far, you may be feeling more confident. You may be able to let go of some baggage that was not only heavy but also unnecessary.

But what about the future?

Is it a case of basking in a lake of self-satisfaction now you're feeling in a better place?

Or is it time to kick on – climb a few more mountains, explore some new landscapes and take a few more people with you for the ride?

Remember the illustration from the first chapter – which day of the week are you on? So what are you going to do with the rest of your journey? Be a player or be a spectator?

The Confidence to Go M.A.D.?

Going M.A.D. is about Making A Difference. Growing in self-confidence will clearly benefit you personally, but wouldn't it be great if it could also benefit others?

I once stayed in a hotel that overlooked Hong Kong harbour. The views were spectacular. The experience was great.

Except for one thing. I had no one to share it with.

Likewise, life is not simply about your journey, but also about how it interplays and influences the journeys of others.

It's now time to explore the connection between confidence and contribution.

Contribution Creates Confidence

As you already know, anxiety occurs when you become overly concerned and sensitive about how you come across to other people. It's possible to obsess about people's opinions of you and to see life as a play where you always have to be centre stage. This constant inward focus becomes unhealthy – and your emotional development is stunted.

Of course, you play the lead role in the drama of your life but even the star of the show spends some time in the wings.

You see, when you turn the spotlight onto others and look to help them, you also develop in the process.

The truth is ...

In helping
others we
help ourselves.

Let's explore in more detail how contribution creates confidence.

The Personal Stuff

Let me tell you about Beth. She's the daughter of one of my best friends. And to me she's an inspiration.

It all started when she watched a video about the work of Operation Christmas Child (www.operationchristmaschild.org.uk). The charity wants Christmas to be a special and exciting time for every child throughout the world, and not just for those who can afford it. In a nutshell, Operation Christmas Child helps ordinary people to make a simple but extraordinary difference to children's lives.

How? The idea is a simple one. Get a shoe box and fill it with some small gifts that are appropriate for either a boy or a girl. There are stipulations on what can and can't be included, but it won't cost much to fill a shoe box.

It's a great idea for many reasons. First, in our household it means we're doing something constructive with all the empty shoe boxes that my teenage daughter Ruth acquires throughout the year.

Secondly, and most importantly, it means that some children wake up at least one day of the year with something very exciting to look forward to. A tangible expression of love, if you like.

Operation Christmas Child provides the ideas, guidance and organisational know-how to make this happen. But that's not enough. The charity also needs people: people to galvanize and inspire others to find and fill those shoe boxes.

And that's where Beth comes in. Beth told her teachers at school about the shoe box campaign. And what did her teachers do?

Told Beth to get on and do it.

They would support her, but as it was her idea she also needed to be the figurehead. They reasoned that a pupil encouraging other pupils to take action was likely to meet with more success than a teacher trying to achieve the same outcome.

Beth was 10 years old at the time. Her primary school mates bought into the idea and the project was a great success.

But it didn't stop there. Beth was so inspired by the simplicity of the idea and the effect it had on children that she wanted to continue the project. She was then 11 and inspired her secondary school to embrace the idea.

"I started small initially," she says. "Just putting up posters around the school and leaflets in class registers. I did a five-minute talk to a year assembly. I was terrified, but Dad gave me some help in what to say."

And the idea grew. As did Beth's confidence.

"My biggest challenge was when I was asked to take the whole school assembly. We showed a video and I talked more about the project."

There were over 900 kids in assembly.

"When I first started doing the assemblies I wrote down everything I wanted to say, but having given a few talks I got to the point whereby I just spoke from the heart."

A 10-year-old Beth never envisaged that her idea would one day see her taking an assembly at secondary school. She simply took the first step. She didn't start with the confidence to do such a thing – the confidence developed as she took the first step.

Maybe that's the key. Don't look at the size of the mountain. Simply focus on the next part of your journey. Start climbing molehills.

The Personal Stuff

In 2003 I went to Tanzania with an organization called Act4Africa. It is a charity that through education and drama helps people in Africa understand and fight against the spread of HIV/AIDS (www.act4africa.org.uk).

The founders of the charity are Martin and Kathy Smedley. Martin's a part-time actor and engineer and Kathy's a teacher. They have teenage kids and a mortgage and seem just like any normal couple.

In fact they are. Except for one thing. They have an overwhelming desire to help prevent the spread of HIV/AIDS in Africa.

That's a tall order.

For an ordinary couple. But they had a belief in themselves that together they could make a difference.

Martin says, "The need is so great we felt we just had to do something – no matter how small. Kathy and I make a good team – our skills complement each other."

Did they possess unshakeable confidence and belief in themselves that they could do something?

"Absolutely not," replied Martin. "We often feel so out of our depth. But if we'd waited until we felt totally confident in our abilities, we'd still be waiting. The crucial thing is just deciding to do something – to take action. Don't let the scale of the problem or your own self-doubt distract you."

Martin and Kathy moved out of their comfortable and safe world in a suburb of Manchester into a world of bureaucracy, red tape and unchartered territory in Africa. They started with no money and no staff, but a belief that together they could do something.

It's been quite a journey. They once found themselves in the Prime Minister's office in Tanzania and have discovered skills they never thought they had: marketing, PR, fund raising and now being seen by others as health experts in the area of HIV/AIDS.

They battle constantly with a need for finances to fund their work, and sometimes wonder if they're really making a difference to such a huge problem.

The facts would suggest they are. So far one million people in Africa have been educated through the Act4Africa programme working in schools, churches and with local community leaders. Their creative approach to tackling the problem is beginning to make a difference.

They have 20 staff – the majority Africans, working long term with their communities. Over 200 people have so far worked with the charity on a short-term basis lasting anywhere from two weeks to a year.

This is not rhetoric. It's reality.

Martin and Kathy's goal was never about how they personally could gain from the experience. It wasn't a strategy to raise their self-esteem and boost their self-confidence.

They simply saw a need and decided to do something about it.

But there have been some additional payoffs to what they have started.

"It's made me realize just how much people are capable of," said Martin. "I'd never have dreamt I could do all the things we've done. Both of us have moved way way out of our comfort zone – and yet we're still standing. I guess our confidence and belief have grown through this whole experience."

So too have the people working with them on a short-term basis. Martin elaborated, "I think it's fair to say we've had some interesting characters join up – and I'm not just thinking of you, Paul! We've had a couple of people with deep psychological problems who'd heard of our work. We took a risk with them. But it's not like we were giving them a full-time job. They've had to raise their own funds to come out and join us on a short-term basis. And they have.

"What's more, the work has provided these people with an outward focus. Rather than always looking inward at their own issues, they've been confronted with other people's problems. We've put some trust in [these] people, given them responsibility, and it's paid off."

One girl who'd been on the team recently qualified as a nurse. She had all sorts of issues when she went out to Tanzania with Martin, and was unemployed at the time. "I guess Act4Africa played some part in her recovery," commented Martin.

What triggered this amazing work?

Desire was definitely at the top of the list. Martin and Kathy felt almost a calling to do something.

But did confidence play a part?

Absolutely.

Without some degree of self-belief nothing would ever have happened.

They knew they had some abilities. They knew they were a good team together. And they knew that the biggest obstacle to overcome was simply to start the work.

Martin and Kathy are remarkable people who continue to face many challenging situations. They've opted out of the kingdom of comfort and decided to make a difference.

And that's exactly what they've done. Not just to a million people in Africa. Not just to 200 people in the UK. But also to themselves.

The truth is ...

When we make a difference to others we also make a difference to ourselves.

Over to you

So you've heard Beth's, Martin's and Kathy's story, and how they're seeking to make a difference.

The question is, what's your story going to be?

I'm not suggesting that you start a charity or move to Africa, but I am suggesting that you take some action. Do something where you're not the focus, but someone or something else is.

The goal is not to broadcast how wonderful you are, but simply to offer your services or implement an idea that will help others.

If you Google "volunteering" you will discover countless websites that can inspire you with ideas on how you can make a difference. The chances are that when you do this you'll be doing something that takes you out of your comfort zone.

The picture could look like this:

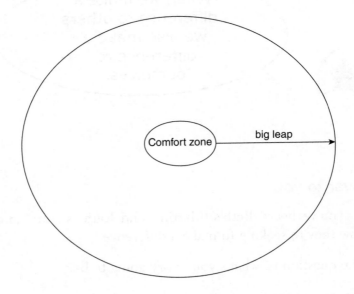

It's a big stretch. You're way out of your comfort zone. For Beth that would have meant starting secondary school and within a matter of weeks taking the whole school assembly.

For Martin and Kathy that would have meant starting a charity and then visiting the Prime Minister's office in Tanzania within a few weeks.

But that didn't happen straight away. It might for some people; but not for Beth, Kathy and Martin.

Moving out of their comfort zone looked more like this:

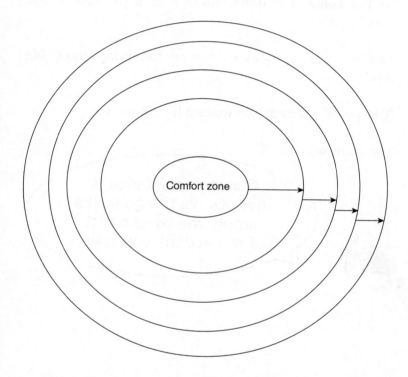

Notice that the first step they took was still the biggest. It's usually the hardest one to take. What follows can often be a series of small steps taken over time.

Each step sees the expanding of their comfort zone. It's not a dramatic leap – that's often not required. But like building a wall, confidence can take time. It's built gradually, one brick at a time.

But as Beth said, "Actually it's amazing looking back how far I've come. You don't realize it until you take a look back."

You see small actions over time can bring about big results.

A 10 percent change can make a big difference.

The truth is ...

> Gaining confidence is not always the goal. It's simply the by-product of the actions you take.

And remember, taking action is rarely done in isolation. Martin and Kathy had each other; Beth found support from her mum and dad and a couple of teachers. Evidence again that you do get by with a little help from your friends.

A Dreamer or a Doer?

Anyone can dream. Lots of people do.

Anyone can have ideas. The world is full of people with ideas.

But the value of dreams and ideas is when you turn them into actions. It's when you take the first step.

I knew I wanted to take my principles developed in my *SUMO* (*Shut Up, Move On*) book into education. My first step?

Mention it in my SUMO book.

That's all.

I had no idea how long it would take to materialize, or even what the product would look like, but I knew I needed people to help turn the dream into a reality. I was overwhelmed with enthusiastic people contacting me, but ultimately I needed enthusiasts who could also be implementers.

It took me two years to find them. And it's been hard work. But in 2009 we launched SUMO4Schools in the UK. Ultimately the goal is to take the concept into other countries as we seek to provide young people with the skills, insights and confidence to make their own difference in life.

Martin Luther King had a dream – but he also had a strategy. He had people alongside him who worked tirelessly to make the dream a reality.

Dreams are the sexy stuff. They're what inspire people. But it's the non-sexy stuff – the phone calls, the planning, the travelling, the printing, the organizing that makes the dreams come true.

Barack Obama's Presidential campaign slogan was "Yes We Can." Interestingly, in a land that worships individualism, he didn't choose "Yes You Can." Working together, collectively, for the benefit of others is what his vision is about.

That's a lesson for us all.

Pit Stop

∞ What part of Beth's and Kathy and Martin's stories inspired you most?

∞ Write down a way in which you make a difference.

∞ If you were to "start small" what would your goal be?

∞ Who would be the "friends" you need to help you?

∞ What's the first action you need to take?

Let me know what you decide to do – contact me at Paul.McGee@theSUMOguy.com.

May you have the confidence to go and make a difference.

And if you feel nervous, anxious or even terrified at the prospect, may you have the courage to take the first step. Feel the fear and go for it anyway.

And here's the remarkable truth. I promise you that a small change, over time, can and will make a difference – not just to you, but to others as well.

I hope that reading this book provides you with some of the tools, encouragement and, perhaps most importantly, the confidence to do so.

Let me know how you get on.

I wish you success.

Go M.A.D.

Paul – The Sumo Guy

How it Worked for Me

Bev, 55, Melbourne

Dear Paul

I am very pleased to say your book has had a great impact on my life and at the age of 55 I have learned and am still learning how to be more confident, deal with stress and approach life with a different attitude. I have learned that I must put myself first; this enables me to be a better wife, mother and friend. Through reading your book, I have learned to stop beating myself up, this has helped immensely with my lack of self-confidence. I was my own worst enemy and never felt I was good at anything, even though I have set up and run my own business for 10 years; and yes it is successful. I decided to take a part-time job for a while to see if someone else would employ me and received a few job offers; much to my surprise! I took up an offer, but after a month and with the aid of reading your book again, I realized that working for myself rather than someone else was actually better for me. I quit my job and with newer insight have been forging ahead in my own business with more vigour than I have had in years. Your book made me realize my thinking was weighing me down, self-criticism had become the norm, so now I turn the switch in my head; to change my thinking from negative to positive. I am not saying this is easy but with practice it is becoming more so;

it is fantastic to know I have the ability to be my own best friend. You have allowed me, to not think that I must be perfect, to realize I am a great person with much to offer. I am happier and yes even though sometimes I wallow, it is never for too long, I have even stopped myself from moaning about the slightest of things. My family has noticed that I moan less and laugh more and although they have always loved me, I am much nicer to be with.

Cheers for now

Bev Ford

Nikki, 32, Cheshire

Reading this book made me finally realize that I'm not perfect, I never will be no matter how hard I punish myself for it and, most importantly, this is OK.

Before reading the book I had recently become a step-mother to two teenage girls and was putting myself under unbelievable pressure to be perfect. Perfect meals, have the perfect house, to put it bluntly I wanted to be the best female role model they could possibly have. This as you can imagine led to tears and frustration on my part.

But Paul's wise words that we can be both flawed and fantastic really struck a chord with me and gave me the confidence to go out and try the things I've always thought I'd fail at. Now if I do fail I think "So what?" I'll just keep on trying until I succeed, and in realising I'm not perfect the pressure to succeed immediately or bid a hasty retreat is gone. This has made a huge difference to the way I feel about myself and the way our family works.

I recently tried a Zumba taster workshop and now regularly attend classes two or three times a week. I would never have done that previously due to embarrassment, wondering what will people think of me – I'm too fat etc. Well I pride myself on being kind and compassionate to others and now know how to be kind and compassionate to myself. That loud booming voice from my inner critic has been reduced to an occasional whisper. I've taken off the boxing glove. I won't allow a lack of self-confidence to steer my life anymore. I've quit the excuses and grabbed hold of the steering wheel – my destination is well and truly in my hands.

Richard, 28, Glasgow

Hi Paul,

I recently bought your *Self-Confidence* book at Edinburgh airport when I was making a trip to Munich last week. The book was a good read and I have been thinking about and using some of the techniques you discuss. I only bought the book by chance for something to read on my flight but the timing of the purchase was excellent as I was due to give a presentation at work the following week.

I would say I am a fairly outgoing and confident person and I bought the book more as a way to take things to the next level – towards B and C as you show on your graph through a 10% change. I liked the breakdown into different actions as I had originally approached the book with a mindset to help improve my confidence for work-related aspects; after reading I appreciated that the techniques could be applied to other parts of my life.

There was one week to go prior to my presentation after reading your book – I decided I would put a plan together as to how I intended to put together, practise and deliver my presentation. As part of this preparation I decided to take on your challenge of creating three phrases I could say to myself to help improve my self-confidence. For the purposes of preparing for my presentation I chose the following three phrases;

1   – "I am doing the correct preparation for a successful presentation"
2   – "I am going to smile during this presentation" (then actually smile after saying it)
3   – "I will ask for and then use constructive criticism and feedback from senior colleagues"

During the days leading up to the presentation I reminded myself to say these phrases, here is a summary of how I think they helped:

1   – When I said this it made me assess whether this statement was true – it made me put more time into

preparing slides and fine tuning of the spoken message. The words correct and successful gave me confidence that I would deliver it well if I did the work I needed to do in preparing the talk.

2   – This made me laugh as it felt a bit silly, however, it did bring focus to something which can easily be forgotten during presentations.

3   – This reminded me that this was a learning experience for me – there is always room to improve, I knew it was not going to be perfect; I am not the finished article. This took the pressure off me as I do tend to put a lot of pressure on myself to try and achieve high standards.

The presentation was yesterday – I spoke without notes for about 30 minutes; my preparation paid off. I was nervous to start and a slight delay didn't help matters, however, once we got going I started to relax into it and knew I was in control. I asked for feedback from my managers later that afternoon and they told me they thought the presentation went well – they gave me some pointers on how to better control the discussions which followed and how to wrap things up at the end.

I intend to put this into practice and also intend to make use of some props in my next presentation, possibly get up there and do some sketching on the wall and walk about to interact with the audience more as I have seen other senior colleagues do.

I enjoyed reading your book and I do hope the 10% I have changed will bring me the long-term rewards that I strive to achieve. The short-term results are certainly evident so a promising 12 months hopefully lies ahead.

Best regards,

Richard

Nadine, 22, Luxembourg

Hi Paul,

Your book did help me quite a lot. I used the following three phrases of the chapter "How to be your own best mate":

1 I recognize I have some failings and I'm still an OK person.
2 I'm making progress from where I was before.
3 I recognize and value the many qualities I have.

They helped me in the way that I finally started to realize that nobody is perfect, and that it is okay to have flaws, but I learned to master them instead of them mastering me. I started thinking about my life more and more and started to recognize my values, but I also found out the reasons for my lack in self-confidence.

My story is that as a kid I was really shy and I didn't talk to anyone. I got bullied at school, and people told me I wasn't normal and wasn't going to make it far in life. Even though my shyness and self-confidence slowly improved over the years, these words always stayed on my mind and occasionally my self-confidence went very low again. All I saw were my own failings, and I thought I wasn't worth anything. I felt insecure and inferior to other people, which was of course partly due to what people thought of me – but also due to what I thought of myself. I only saw what I couldn't do, but not what I could.

A few years ago, though, it became my dream to study at a university in England.

People said I wouldn't make it, but as it says in your book I decided to be the driver of my life and prove them wrong.

I sent applications to five universities. Filling in the application form made me recognize some of my qualities. I am quite good at languages. I speak five languages fluently. I got unconditional offers from four of them.

I have still had moments of self-doubt, but now I don't allow them to master me.

I have now moved from Luxembourg to study in London. I AM making my dream come true. If someone had told me that a few years ago, I wouldn't have believed them. But the shy Nadine has actually gone to England all on her own. Sometimes I take it for granted, or I think it's not that special. Sometimes I think I was just lucky.

But your book reminded me that everyone is responsible for their own destiny. I took action, and I made it happen. Your book also helped me realize that I have been a fighter all my life. I often used to feel down because of what people made me feel like, and as I've said, I felt worthless. I often fell. But I remembered that no matter how low I felt, I never gave up. I always stood up again, and I fought for my dreams.

I want to thank you again for the inspiration your book gave me, and for the realisations I made by reading it.

All the best,

Nadine

More Stuff That Will Help

The Jelly Effect – How To Make Your Communication Stick,
Andy Bounds – Capstone Publishing, 2007

How to Win Friends and Influence People, Dale Carnegie –
Vermillion, 2007

How to Stop Worrying And Start Living, Dale Carnegie –
Cedar, 1993

*How to Talk to Anyone: 92 Little Tricks For Big Success in Rela-
tionships,* Leil Lowndes – Thorsons, 2008

Great Answers To Tough Interview Questions, Martin John
Yate – Kogan Page, 2008

Cognitive Behavioural Therapy For Dummies, Rob Wilson and
Rhena Branch – John Wiley and Sons, 2005

Being Happy! A Handbook To Greater Confidence and Security,
Andrew Matthews – Media Masters, 1989

Instant Confidence, Paul McKenna – Bantam Press, 2006

And a few more from Paul McGee

How To Write a CV That Really Works, How To Books, 2009

S.U.M.O. Shut Up, Move On. The Straight Talking Guide to Creating and Enjoying a Brilliant Life, Capstone Publishing, 2006

S.U.M.O. Your Relationships. How to Handle Not Strangle The People You Live and Work With, Capstone Publishing, 2007

59 Minutes to a Calmer Life. Go MAD Books, 2001

Time for Some Gratitude

If there's one lesson I learnt in life it's this: success comes from the support of others. I'm a living example of how true that is.

So it's time to publicly acknowledge some of the supporters who've helped contribute to my journey so far and who've given me the confidence to pursue some of my dreams.

Andy Bounds and Richard Farrow have both taken time to give their invaluable insights as to how to improve this book. I'm truly grateful for your wisdom and fresh perspective. Thanks guys.

As for Mr Sandham, well it still concerns me that you know more about Russian literature than you do football, but I still love you (in the brotherly sense). Thanks for being such a key player in my life and for so graciously pointing out my many blind spots. I've grown in confidence because of you.

Andy and Gill, your passion for SUMO4Schools is inspiring. Thank you for all your energy and commitment to help turn a dream into a reality. Your friendship is invaluable and your kids are adorable. Pity about your football team though.

To my friends at Eagles in Singapore, well you've become a second family to me. Thank you for the faith you've shown in me and for the fun we've had together. Your hospitality and generosity has both humbled my heart and widened my waistline.

As for my professional speaking buddies well your support, wisdom and advice has been priceless. Special thanks go to Dave Thomas, Brendan Power, Will Kintish, Roy Sheppard, Phil Hesketh, Steve McDermott, Curly Uppington, Clive Gott, John Hotowka, Damian Hughes, Shay McConnon, Molly Harvey, Frank Furness, Amanda Clarke, Val McKie, Marie Mosley, Lesley Everett, Nigel Risner, Robin Sieger, Steve Head, Paul Bridle and Bill Dougherty. Keep making a difference guys.

Mark and Anita you've become very special friends in such a short period of time. You've been my cheerleaders and your generosity, humour and passion for life is infectious. It's a privilege knowing you both.

To Commander Ken and gorgeous Gail I thank you again for laughter, good wine, long walks (!) and your willingness to listen to my stories. How gracious you are.

J. John you're amazing. You personify for me the gift of encouragement. Your integrity, faithfulness and desire to do all you can to help others succeed and find meaning in life, is an example to us all.

As for Richard and Fiona, you simply excel in encouragement. You've built me up so much over the years and your willingness to help others is inspiring. Thank you.

Special thanks also to my editor Holly Bennion – those long conversations have been worth it. And to Kev Daniels who worked tirelessly typing up this manuscript and deciphering my scrawl – you deserve a medal. Thanks for becoming such an integral part of the SUMO team.

As for Graham Britton – I've rarely come across anyone who is as professional and reliable as you. Thanks for all your dedication and hard work mate.

To my brother Andy I have only one question. How come you got the good looks, height and super-efficient metabolic rate? Still love you though and appreciate your wealth of wisdom that you're so willing to share. Still struggle that you support Manchester City though.

Mum and Dad I'm so grateful that on a cold winter's night back in '63 you decided to switch off the TV and have an early night. Hopefully what happened nine months later made it worthwhile! Mum keep being a glamorous Nan and Dad keep telling your stories (but get a new hearing aid – please!).

Margaret you're not just a great ironer, decorator and cat sitter – you're a pretty good mother-in-law as well. Thanks for bearing with my humour.

And finally to Helen, Matt and Ruth. What can I say? I'm proud to be your husband and father. You make my life complete guys and I'll be eternally grateful for having you around – particularly when I need to erect some flat-packed furniture or learn how to operate some new technical gadget. (Admit it though – I did pretty well learning how to use the new toaster.)

With gratitude

Paul McGee

Bring Paul McGee to Your Organisation

Paul McGee speaks around the world at team events, conferences, workshops and retreats. From a one hour keynote presentation, to a three day seminar, Paul tailors his material to your specific requirements, primarily in the areas of:

∞ Change
∞ Relationships
∞ Attitude
∞ Motivation
∞ Stress
∞ Confidence
∞ Leadership
∞ Customer Service

In order to make contact with Paul or to learn more about **SUMO4Schools**

email

Paul.McGee@theSUMOguy.com

visit

www.TheSumoGuy.com

or telephone

+44(0) 1925 268708

Follow Paul on Twitter: @TheSumoGuy

Index

ability 19–22, 30–1, 37, 44
achievements, identifying
146–8, 174
Act4Africa 257–261
action 135–9, 149, 213, 221–2
Coaches 106
making a difference
253–267
T.E.A.R. process 88, 101–2
aggression 225, 227–9
Aggressors 227–9, 245
alcohol 43–4, 45, 250
anxiety 135, 138, 152–161, 254
dating 177–180
F.A.T. method 159
public speaking 162, 166
appearance 182–184
applying for jobs 13, 15, 85, 103
interviews 168–176
approval, seeking 232–3
arousal 157

arrogance 37, 115, 171, 175
Avoiders 225–7
Awfulisers 59–64, 206

bad news 83–87, 153–154
Beck, Aaron 89
beliefs 50–4, 73, 76, 133
influences on 54–64, 82–3
living up to
accomplishments 66
negative 90, 92–93, 94, 130,
191
see also thinking
bicycle, learning to ride a
134–5
Blair, Tony 165
"Blame Game" 50, 60, 73
bosses 101
bouncing back 218–220
boundaries, setting clear 234,
235

Index

Bounds, Andy 118
brain processes 153–5, 157, 195
bullying 225, 274
bungee jumping 138–9

Cantona, Eric 7
Challengers 104–106, 112–18
change, effect of 16–18, 23–4, 27
charity work 255–61
Cheerleaders 101–103, 112–16, 215, 251
children 68–72
  Cheerleader role of parents 115
  influence of upbringing 55–8
  mixed messages given to 66
  over-protectiveness towards 61–3
Clinton, Bill 165
clothes 183–4, 221
Coaches 106–109, 113, 114, 117–118
cognitive behavioural therapy (CBT) 89, 131
comfort zone 152, 195, 262–263
communication 224, 236
compassion 128–129, 271
competence 30–2, 36, 44
complacency 41, 115, 251

compliments 185
conference presentations 14, 15, 16, 161–168, 272–3
Confidants 109–112, 113, 114, 117, 206, 215
conflict 223–48
  aggression 227–9
  avoidance of 225–7
  focus on facts 239–40
  insights into 230–7
  preparation for an uncomfortable conversation 237–8
  saving face 240
  solution focus 241–2
contribution 254–267
control, taking 132–134, 149, 271
conversations, uncomfortable 237–43, 244
criticism 65, 69, 139–142
  constructive 272
  defensiveness 240
  self-criticism 128–31, 190–1, 251, 269
Cruise, Tom 12–13

dating 14, 15, 177–195
defensiveness 240, 246
delusion 31
demands, unreasonable 236–7
Denny, Richard 38
dinner dates 180

divorce 214–215
dreams 265–266, 276
dress 182–184, 221

emotions (feelings) 208–211,
    222, 252
    anxious 159, 160
    brain processes 154
    conflict 239
    grieving 203–204
    stories 165
    T.E.A.R. process 88, 89,
        101–2
encouragement 19, 33, 35, 94,
    101
exams 71
experience 35, 36
    influence of past
        experiences 48–9, 73
    learning from 192, 194,
        216–217, 252
"Explain Game" 50–64, 73,
    250
extroverts 32–3

face, saving 240
F.A.T. method 159
fear 158
feedback 141–2, 272, 273
feelings see emotions
flaws 124–127, 149, 251, 274
friends 98, 101, 117–18,
    119–121, 206, 264

Gallup 148
grieving 201–205, 219, 252
guilt 234

height 12–13
help 97–121, 215, 255, 264
How to Write a C.V. that Really
    Works (McGee) 176
humility 36–7, 40, 44, 213

ice breakers 21
ill health 199–200, 205, 217
independence 99
influences
    external 75–94
    past 47–65, 250
insecurity 93, 232–3
inspiration 119, 255–257,
    266
interest, showing 186, 189
interviews 85, 168–176
introverts 32–3

job loss 85–7, 200–1
job-seeking 13, 15, 85, 103
    interviews 168–176

King, Martin Luther 165,
    265

labels 144
lies 51–4
life course 24–5

making a difference (M.A.D.)
    253–267
McGee, Andy 177, 193–195
McGee, Helen 81, 118, 181,
    199, 201, 206, 217, 244–7
media 82–87, 94
memory 154
mistakes 70, 142–3, 250
    admitting 36–7
    learning from 243
mothers 19, 56, 59–61, 63, 78,
    116
    see also parents
motivation 174

needs 125
nerves 136, 156–157, 190, 195
news 83–87
"no", saying 233–4

Obama, Barack 266
Operation Christmas Child
    255–7
opinions, expressing your 233
opportunity 20–2, 26, 38
over-protectiveness 61–3

Page, David 51–2
parents 49, 55–63, 69–71, 73,
    99, 101
    Cheerleader role 115
    encouragement from 19,
    35

mixed messages from 66
over-protectiveness 61–3
past influences 47–65, 250
perfection 126–127, 149,
    270
personal development 38–40
personality, innate 32–4
perspective 207–208, 211–12
politics 21
potential, unfulfilled 31–2,
    93
PowerPoint 164
practice 167
preparation
    job interviews 169–171
    public speaking 166,
    272–3
    uncomfortable
        conversations 237–8
presentations 14, 15, 16,
    161–168, 272–3
pride 213–215, 222
problems 211–212, 215
public speaking 14, 15, 16,
    19–21, 161–168, 272–3

Question Time 20–1

racism, accusations of 141–2
Rath, Tom 148
recovery 201–221, 251
Redgrave, Steven 100
reflection 49–50, 190–191

rejection 155, 174, 190–3
relationships
  breakdown 202, 214
  conflict 229, 248
  initiating 14, 15
  see also dating
relaxation 160
respect 193–4, 235
responsibilities 235–7, 248
rights 232–5, 248
Robbins, Anthony 211
Rohn, John 175
romance see dating

salesmanship 172–174
Sartre, Jean Paul 165
school 76–82, 94, 274
Scum (film) 181
self-criticism 128–31, 190–1,
  251, 269
self-deprecation 92–93, 190
self-doubt 41–3, 45, 224,
  250, 275
self-harm, psychological
  131
self-help publications and
  speakers 30, 38, 40
self-respect 174
self-worth 65, 67, 72, 73,
  275, 276
setbacks 197–222, 252
shyness 274–5
situations 34–6, 250

skills
  communication 224
  identifying your 144–6
Skinner, Frank 41–2
Smedley, Martin and Kathy
  258–261, 262–263, 264,
  266
solutions, focus on 241–2
S.T.A.R. method 147–8
stock take, success 142–8,
  149
stories 164–165
Strengths Finder 2.0 (Rath)
  148
stress 155–156
success stock take 142–8,
  149
S.U.M.O. (Shut Up, Move On)
  (McGee) 64, 88, 116, 265
Sumo4Schools 118, 265
support 97–121, 213–214,
  215, 264
survival 154–155

talent 19–22
teachers 76–82, 94, 101, 109
T.E.A.R. process 88–89,
  101–102, 106
Thatcher, Margaret 231
thinking 88, 89, 101–2
  see also beliefs
"Thinking", poem 120–1
threat 154–155

Index

upbringing 54–64
  see also children

visualization 159–160
volunteering 261–262

Washington, Denzel 76
weight 18, 55–7, 83, 147–8
Whittaker, Rob 50–1, 52
Wintle, Walter D. 121
Woods, Tiger 167

yeast 18
yourself
  helping 123–149
  relationship with 251
  talking to 88–91, 131–132,
    252
  undermining 87–94
  valuing 72–3
  see also self-criticism;
    self-doubt; self-worth